CW00621349

HC
POCKET BOOK

House Beautiful

HOMEFAX
POCKET BOOK

Edited by
Pat Roberts and Caroline Atkins

VERMILION
LONDON

First published in 1992 in Great Britain by Vermilion
an imprint of the Random Century Group
Random Century House
20 Vauxhall Bridge Road
London SW1V 2SA

British Library Cataloguing-in-Publication Data
A catalogue record for this book is available from the British
Library.

ISBN 0 085223 824 X

Cover design: Slatter Anderson

Additional material supplied by: Martin Johnson, Barty Phillips,
Ann Scutcher, Nicole Swengley, Susan Welby.

Illustrations: Susannah English, Val Hill,
Lesley Sage, Axel Scheffler.

Printed and bound by Clays Ltd, St Ives plc.

The editors would like to state that the information contained
in this book was checked as rigorously as possible before
going to press. Neither the editors nor the publisher can
take responsibility for any changes which may have occurred
since, nor for any other variance of fact from that recorded
here in good faith.

CONTENTS

BASIC HOME TOOL KIT

The following items make up a basic household kit for essential repairs and DIY. Keep small tools in a tool box or canvas bag or on organised wall storage in the garage. If you're buying a new set of tools, it's worth paying for good ones – they are easier to use and last longer. But remember that some of the simplest household objects – such as wire coat-hangers – can prove surprisingly useful in an emergency. ALWAYS put tools away when you have finished with them. Keep ladders locked up.

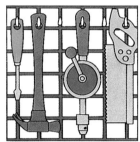

1 **Aluminium steps** for changing light bulbs, decorating, climbing up to tall shelves, cleaning windows, hanging pictures.

2 **Claw hammer** for pulling out and knocking in nails, picture hooks etc.

3 **General-purpose pliers** with partly serrated jaws for gripping flat objects and partly curved jaws for gripping rods. Choose a pair with plastic insulated handles.

4 **Screwdrivers** in various sizes. You will need a set of

BASIC HOME TOOL KIT

cross-headed screwdrivers in graded sizes and a set of flat-bladed ones including very small ones for electric plugs. Stubby-handled ones are good for working in confined spaces.

5 **Wire strippers** for changing plugs.

6 **Saw** A tenon saw (one with a rigid back) is the most versatile.

7 **Electric drill** and set of bits. Hand drills are often

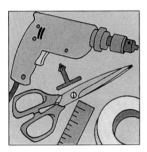

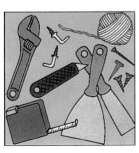

said to be easier for beginners, but they require pressure and weight as well as correct aim, so many, in fact, find an electric one more helpful.

8 **Bradawl and gimlet** to make starter-holes in walls or woodwork for screws, nails, cup hooks etc.

9 **Adjustable spanner**.

10 **DIY knife** with retractable blade.

11 **Steel rule** and measuring tape in both metric and imperial units.

12 **Wire coat-hanger(s)** for drain cleaning, loo unblocking, fishing car keys out of drains and other invaluable uses.

13 **Plunger** for clearing blocked sinks.

14 **Nails and screws**, picture hooks and cup hooks in various sizes and lengths.

15 **String and rope**.

16 **Sticky tapes**, including insulating tape, masking tape and carpet tape.

17 **General-purpose scissors** to cut paper and other 'blunting' materials. Don't use good scissors for paper as it will blunt them.

18 **Wall plugs** for solid walls.

19 **Paint and wallpaper scrapers**.

20 **Ladder** for roof maintenance, gutters etc.

GUIDE TO PAINT TYPES

All paints on the market, whatever their trade name, fall into one of two main categories – gloss or emulsion. Gloss paints are oil-based and soluble with white spirit. Emulsion paints are water-soluble. Follow our guide to match the right paint to the job.

Liquid gloss: Very shiny finish. Needs an undercoat. Seal bare wood with a primer first. (If possible use a combined primer and undercoat as this will save drying time.) Liquid gloss is mainly used for wood and metal (eg radiators). Coverage per litre: 17sq m.

Non-drip gloss: High-shine finish. Has a gelatinous texture and will not drip or run. Does not require an undercoat, but you must prime bare wood before you apply it. Mainly used for wood and metal, and also good for plastic surfaces such as guttering and drainpipes. Coverage per litre: 12-15sq m.

Self-undercoating gloss: This combines the qualities of liquid and non-drip gloss Has a thick, creamy consistency and dries to a high-shine finish. Covers most colours with a single coat. It is used for wood, metal and plastic. Coverage per litre: 10sq m.

Mid-sheen oil-based paints: Commonly known as Eggshell, although Dulux call theirs Satinwood. Soft-sheen finish. Less tough that gloss and harder to keep clean. These paints do not need an undercoat but will usually require two or more coats to cover properly. Bare wood will need priming first. Can be used on walls, or as a more subtle alternative to gloss for woodwork and metal. Coverage per litre: 16sq m.

Vinyl silk emulsion: Silky, low-sheen finish. Does not need undercoat. Good for damp, steamy walls in kitchens and

GUIDE TO PAINT TYPES

bathrooms as it can be wiped clean. The silky finish emphasises flaws but is good for highlighting the design of relief-pattern wall coverings. Suitable for walls and ceilings. Coverage per litre: 13-14sq m.

Vinyl matt emulsion: Soft, matt finish. Does not need undercoat. The most common choice for walls and ceilings. Helps disguise uneven surfaces. Coverage per litre: 14-15sq m.

Solid emulsion/Roller paint: Available in both matt and silk finishes. Does not need undercoat. Comes packaged in its own paint tray ready to use. Designed for use on walls and ceilings. The range of colours available is limited. The texture is thick, so the paint won't drip or run. Coverage per litre: 12sq m.

One-coat paints: Available in emulsion, gloss and satin finishes. Self-undercoating and very opaque, so one coat will obliterate most colours. The

thick, creamy consistency means quicker application, less tendency to run and it will fill hairline cracks, so less preparation work is needed. Coverage per litre: 10sq m.

Dulux Kitchens & Bathrooms Paint: Silky, low-sheen finish. Basically an emulsion but the high acrylic content makes it more washable and a mild fungicide guards against mould growth caused by condensation. Coverage per litre: 16sq m.

Note: Remember that paint will dry a slightly different colour from the shade it appears as you apply it wet. It's best to try out your choice on a small test area before you tackle a whole wall. Small sampler pots are available for most ranges, which come complete with an integral brush and give you enough paint to try out two coats of your colour an an area of about 1sq ft.

HANGING WALL COVERINGS

1 For unpasted vinyl wall coverings, mix paste according to packet instructions. Place your first length of paper face down on the pasting table. Use a pasting brush to paste along the entire length, working it outwards to ensure the edges are covered. Fold pasted surfaces together, bringing top and bottom to meet in the middle. For longer lengths fold like a concertina.

the ceiling line for trimming, then slide the paper into position at the plumb line. Smooth down the middle of the paper with a paper-hanger's brush, working out towards the edges to remove any air bubbles.

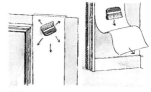

5 Unfold the rest of the paper and continue to smooth down, leaving a trimming margin of 5cm at the bottom of the wall.

2 For pre-pasted vinyls, simply immerse the cut length, rolled up, in tepid water for ten seconds – ask your retailer for a water trough – then slowly unroll to ensure all the pre-pasted back is saturated.

3 Before starting to hang your wall covering, ensure that the walls are sound, clean and dry. Drop a plumb line at a convenient place to start your decoration.

4 Carry the pasted paper to the wall, open the top fold and stick the top half of the length on the wall. Allow 5cm extra at

6 With a straightedge and sharp knife, trim the paper along the angles of the ceiling and the skirting to give a neat finish. Wipe off excess paste with a damp sponge, and brush down the edges of the paper.

7 Position the next length of paper on the wall beside the first. Slide it into place to butt up to, but not overlap, the first length, and so that the pattern matches at eye level. If wrinkles appear, there are still air pockets under the paper. Gently peel the paper back and brush it down again. Minor wrinkles will disappear on drying.

HANGING WALL COVERINGS

8 If necessary, gently use a seam roller to flatten joins about 20 minutes after hanging. (Don't roll blown or flock vinyls.)

and sharp knife, cut through the overlap, remove surplus underneath and press two edges together.

9 Never hang a full width of paper round a corner; always hang it in two parts. First measure the distance from the last piece you have hung to the corner. Do this at several points from skirting to ceiling to find the greatest distance.

10 Cut a strip of paper 2cm *wider* than this distance and hang it with the extra 2cm overlapping onto the next wall. Measure the width of the offcut from the corner and mark a vertical this distance from the corner onto the side wall. Paste the offcut, aligning the uncut edge with the vertical line so that the cut edge overlaps the first piece. With a straightedge

11 Before papering round a light switch, turn off electricity at mains. For best results, remove the fitting and replace after papering. If this isn't possible, for a square fitting, pierce paper at centre of fitting and make four diagonal cuts to approx 2.5cm beyond each corner. (Make star-shaped cuts for a round fitting.)

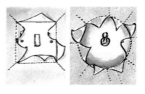

12 Press around edge of fitting. Trim away excess, leaving 3mm-4mm extra all round. Unscrew the plate, brush extra paper behind it and screw back into place again. (With metallic wall coverings, which could conduct electricity, cut to fit *around* the switch.)

FLOOR MAINTENANCE

**PATCHING A RUG
TOOLS AND MATERIALS
Latex carpet adhesive –**

**Copydex is good; DIY
knife or sharp scissors;
spare carpet; hessian.**

1 Use a piece of leftover carpet or take a piece from a hidden area under the bed or another large piece of furniture.

2 Lay the piece on top of the damaged carpet, matching up pattern, pile or grain, and cut through both together with a DIY knife or sharp scissors.

3 Stop any fraying by putting latex adhesive along the edges of hole and patch to halfway up the pile. Leave to dry until semi-transparent.

4 Fit the patch into the hole.

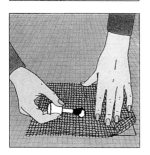

5 Cut a piece of hessian slightly larger than the patch, turn the rug over and stick the hessian over the back with latex adhesive. Tap with a hammer to make sure it sticks.

FLOOR MAINTENANCE

PATCHING FITTED CARPET OR LINOLEUM

TOOLS AND MATERIALS
Small piece of lining paper; other items as listed for *Patching a Rug* – see over.

1 These have to be patched in situ, from the top. Cut out the patch and the damaged piece together (see step 2 of **Patching a Rug**).

2 Cut a piece of paper slightly larger than the patch and push it through the hole to lie flat on the floor or underfelt.

3 Cut a piece of hessian smaller than the paper but slightly larger than the hole and push it through the hole to lie on top of the paper.

4 Paste latex adhesive on the exposed piece of hessian.

5 Put the patch in position and tap round the edges with a hammer to make sure it bonds.

PATCHING VINYL FLOORING

TOOLS AND MATERIALS
Heavy-duty, double-sided adhesive tape (e.g. Copydex Heavy Duty Double Sided); other items as for *Patching a Rug*.

1 Lift the vinyl and work from underneath. Brush and vacuum both vinyl and floor well.

2 Cut out the patch and the damaged piece together (see step 2 of **Patching a Rug**).

3 Use tape to fix the underside of the patch and the back of the main piece of vinyl to the floor.

FLOOR MAINTENANCE

BINDING MATTING

Sisal, cord and coconut matting will fray at the edges unless they have a satisfactory latex border on both sides of the matting. You can bind any small rug or carpet this way, but ensure it is completely clean, or adhesive won't stick.

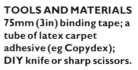

TOOLS AND MATERIALS
75mm (3in) binding tape; a tube of latex carpet adhesive (eg Copydex); DIY knife or sharp scissors.

1 Trim the edges with a DIY knife or sharp scissors.

2 Cut the tape to the required length and squeeze or paint the latex adhesive along half the width of the tape and to the same width along one edge of the matting. When nearly dry, stick the two coated sides together.

3 Turn the matting over and repeat the process with the other half of the tape.

4 Tap along both sides with a hammer to make sure it bonds.

FLOOR MAINTENANCE

MOVING A STAIR CARPET

Stair carpets moved from time to time will wear more evenly. Use one-piece carpet grippers, available in three lengths.

1 Take up the carpet.

2 Nail the carpet grippers into the angle of each step.

3 Starting at the top, move the carpet down about 3in from its old position and tack it into place on the riser.

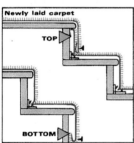

Newly laid carpet

TOP

BOTTOM

After several moves

TOP

BOTTOM

4 A fitting tool should be provided to help you press the carpet firmly onto the gripper pins. Pull it taut over the step, down the riser and on to the next gripper pins, until you reach the bottom.

5 Turn in the surplus at the bottom and tack it under.

The carpet can be lifted and laid again whenever necessary. (Move it up or down according to where you have more surplus.)

SANDING FLOORBOARDS

NOTE: It is advisable to wear a dust mask while sanding. Buy a pack of disposable masks from DIY suppliers ● If you are sanding an upstairs room, remember the dust will settle on the floor below, so you should remove or cover furniture there too ● Be considerate to neighbours – tell them what you are doing and use the sander at a reasonable hour ● If you have a leasehold property, check that you are allowed to carry out the work.

TOOLS AND MATERIALS
Large floor sander (from hire shops); medium and fine-grade sandpaper (available with sander); handscraper or sanding attachment of electric drill for edges and corners; hammer; gloss or matt seal, varnish or wood stain.

1 **Try to get all furniture** and shelving out of the room – sanding produces a lot of dust, even with a dust bag.
2 **Hammer in nails** well below the surface. Split or damaged boards should be replaced. If there are wide gaps, fill with newspaper and wood filler or papier-mâché, or wood slivers.
3 **Use coarse abrasive paper** in the machine to begin (stiff abrasive paper can be rolled in your hands until it becomes easier to fit into the machine). Before switching on, tilt the sander backwards to lift the drum off the floor. Switch on and lower the machine gently. Keep it moving; keep the cable out of the way by running it over your shoulder. Work slowly and evenly and keep control of the machine – it will try to run away with you.

SANDING FLOORBOARDS

4 If floor is badly damaged, go over it diagonally for the first couple of times and then go in the direction of the boards. DO NOT sand at right-angles to the boards.

5 Lift drum off the floor approximately 1m (3ft) before you reach the wall, lower it and pull the sander back along the length you have just done. Always lift the drum before turning for the next stretch.

SEALING

1 Vacuum thoroughly before beginning to apply your varnish or seal.

2 Apply the first coat with a lint-free cloth or sponge or a paint roller, to make sure it sinks into the boards. Subsequent coats can be applied with a brush. Apply two coats in rooms which will have rugs or carpets, and three in hard-worked areas such as the hall or kitchen.

CURING A STICKING DOOR

Several problems may prevent a door from closing properly. They are usually quite simple to deal with.

Never move hinges to a different position.

If the screws won't tighten, use larger ones. Alternatively, wedge the door open at right angles to the frame, remove the screws, fill screw holes with plastic wood and when it has hardened screw them back in firmly.

If the hinges have become too deeply recessed in the wood, unscrew the deeper side, slip a piece of card behind it and screw back again.

If the recesses are too shallow, deepen them slightly with a wood chisel.

I Unscrew the hinges and take the door off.
2 Smooth the wood down at the hinge side and/or the top until the door will fit the frame – allowing for a new coat of paint to be added.

3 Repaint and replace the door on its hinges.
Wood is less likely to swell if it is thoroughly painted, particularly along the edges and the base.

I Find out where the door is sticking either by looking for worn paint, or by chalking the edge and seeing where chalk rubs off when door is closed.
2 Sand or plane the warped wood until the door closes well. Repaint.

CURING A STICKING DOOR

FLOOR COVERING
TOO DEEP

Replace hinges with rising-butt hinges which will lift the door as it opens and closes. (Note: this will only solve the problem if the floor covering is not laid too close to the door.) Rising-butt hinges are in two parts: one fits to the door, the other to the frame.

1 Unscrew the old hinges.
2 Remove the door. Sand (or saw) part of the inner top corner of the door, to accommodate new hinge. (If about to lay new floor covering, place a strip of wood the same thickness as the new flooring against top of door, to mark a sawing line.)
3 Screw the spindle part of the hinge to the frame and the other part to the door.
4 Repaint door where necessary. If it is still tight, plane door at bottom.
Note: Rising-butt hinges need regular lubrication (just a drop of oil at the top).

LAYERS OF PAINT

Paint may build up over the years to make a door stick.
1 Use a paint stripper to remove all old paint.
2 Sandpaper or plane smooth.
3 Prime and repaint.

STIFF HINGES
Metal hinges Apply a drop of oil at the top.
Nylon hinges Slacken or tighten the screws a little.

PUTTING UP SHELVES

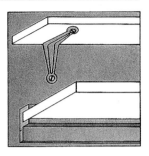

NOTE: To make sure that your shelf will be secure, check that the wall is sound and dry. The thicker the shelves, the more weight they will hold. The distance needed between the supports to prevent shelves from bowing depends on what they will be used for and what they're made of:

15mm (⅝in) hardwood: support every 50cm (20in).
18mm (¾in) plywood: support every 80cm (30in).
12mm (½in) blockboard: support every 45cm (18in).
18mm (¾in) MDF: support every 70cm (27in).
18mm (¾in) melamine-covered chipboard: support every 50cm (20in).
10mm (⅜in) glass: support every 70cm (27in).

TOOLS
Drill, wall plugs, bradawl, plumb-line, spirit level.

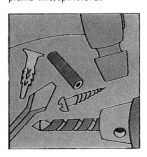

SUPPORT SYSTEMS
Various methods of supporting shelves are available:
● Individual non-adjustable metal brackets, ranging from the very cheap and basic to ornamental wrought iron.
● Individual non-adjustable horizontal strips of metal or wood. The shelf either rests on them or slots into them.
● Metal uprights with adjustable brackets available in different lengths to hold different depths of shelf.
● Wooden adjustable shelving with dowel supports: suitable for display shelving because the supports are almost invisible.

WALL FIXINGS
NOTE: Make sure you don't drill into wires or pipes inside the wall. If fixing shelves to plasterboard, do not use them to hold anything heavy.
Solid walls: Drill a hole for

PUTTING UP SHELVES

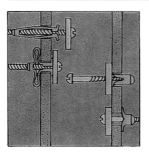

the screw, then plug with a suitable size of fibre or nylon wallplug to give a good grip.
Hollow walls: Screw the brackets into load-bearing struts. Timber uprights (studs) are usually 40cm-45cm (16in-18in) apart, covered with plasterboard. To find them, either tap along the wall with a hammer or use a bradawl. Various wallplugs and toggles are available for hollow walls. Some expand to grip the inside of the wall when the screw is in place, while others have arms which drop down when the bolt is through.

UPRIGHTS AND BRACKETS
This job is far easier if you get a friend to help.

1 Work out where you want your two uprights, and fix the top of one loosely to the wall.
2 Hang a plumb-line (or stone tied to a piece of string) from the top to align the upright vertically and mark the point for the bottom screw.
3 Clip a pair of brackets into position at equal levels on the two uprights. Ask a friend to hold the second upright against the wall while you lay a shelf across the brackets and check the horizontal with a spirit level.
4 Now mark the final screw positions.

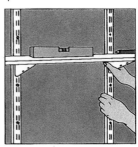

NOTES
● Use a spirit level to check that individual brackets are correctly positioned.
● Screw brackets to shelves to prevent them from overbalancing.
● To finish long shelves, add end boards to hold books etc in place.
● To make a shelf look more substantial, fix a strip of hardwood along the front to form a lip.

GUTTERS AND GULLEYS

SAFETY RULES

● Use a sound ladder, firmly and securely placed.
● Stand ladder on hardboard or chipboard so it won't slip.
● Check ladder extension is firmly fixed.
● Ladder should reach at least 1m (3.3ft) above the highest level at which you want to stand.
● Never stand above the third highest rung.
● Don't lean over the side of the ladder as you work.
● Wear soft-soled shoes with good grip.

CLEANING GUTTERS

1 Clear debris (birds' nests, leaves, moss etc) by scraping gutters with a trowel (debris makes good compost).

2 Hose gutter down if necessary.
3 Check all gutters and downpipes are in good structural condition.
4 Mend minor cracks with waterproof tape.

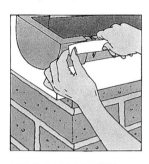

MENDING SAGGING GUTTERS

1 Stretch a length of string along gutter top.
2 Hold spirit level flush with string and check gutter slopes evenly to downpipe.
3 If there's a slight sag, hammer nails into fascia near the outlet, 25mm (1in) below the gutter.

GUTTERS AND GULLEYS

4 Drop gutter to new nails.

5 Make pilot holes for screws with a bradawl. Screw gutter into place.

6 Pour water through and check slope of gutter.

7 Fill holes, prime and paint.

SECURING LOOSE DOWNPIPES

I Lever nails from lowest bracket with claw hammer. Take off downpipe section. Carry on in sections until you reach loose bracket.

2 Make softwood plugs, a little larger and thicker than the holes, and press into holes.

3 Replace downpipe and drive nails through lugs into softwood plugs.

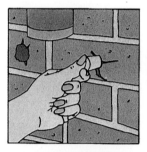

4 If joints between downpipe sections are loose, pack them with proprietary mastic and seal with bitumen paint.

GULLEYS

A gulley is an open rainwater drain in the ground, with a grid. Gulleys should be cleared regularly.

I Scoop out all the old leaves, silt and mud.

2 Wash out the grid with an old scrubbing or washing-up brush.

3 Pour a bucket of water down the gulley.

ROOF CARE

LOFT INSULATION

Loft insulation usually pays for itself within three years. You may be eligible for a grant. Glass fibre and spun mineral wool, from DIY or hardware shops, are easiest. Use rolls of at least 75mm (3in) thick. Use loose fill for filling in awkward spaces or unevenly spaced joists. When covering pipes and working in the eaves, lay cardboard or building paper first.

Tools and materials

Insulating material, small saw, scissors, torch or inspection lamp, long extension lead, piece of wood for pressing material into corners.

● If using glass fibre, wear gloves and a mask.

● Take accurate measurements of space between joists, lengths of joists and the number of spaces between.

● Note size of water tank and length and size of pipes.

● Span joists with wide board to act as working platform.

● Unwrap rolls in loft and work gently to prevent loose fibres blowing about.

● Cut material to fit space between joists and press down to fit snugly.

● Check for frayed wiring and don't cover wiring with insulation.

● Lay insulation *over* pipes, not under them.

● Don't insulate the space under the water tank.

● Rinse hands in cold water before washing, to reduce irritation.

SLATES AND TILES

● Check the roof for any broken slates and tiles that need replacing.

● Slates are secured with strips of lead nailed to the roof batten (see above).

ROOF CARE

● When sliding new slate in place (see right), keep it flat against batten, then hook lead over slate end.

● Tiles may be nailed onto roof battens, or may have 'nibs' which fit over battens.

● Check battens before laying new slates or tiles.

● Hinge up overlapping tiles or slates while working and then hinge down again gently over the new one.

FLAT ROOFS

Note: Good-quality materials are essential for flat roofs because of drainage problems. A flat roof may leak because the covering is cracked by heat or movement of timbers.

● Wear soft-soled shoes when working on roof.

● Remove damaged felt (see right) and check all boards.

● Sweep roof before and after laying underlay and felt.

● After repair, coat roof with mastic and sprinkle white chippings over to reflect heat.

● Stagger successive layers of felt (see right).

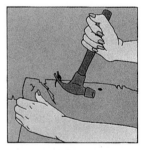

FLASHINGS

These are strips of waterproof material shaped to fit the angle between wall and roof. Zinc is cheap and durable; use it to replace old mortar flashing in the roof/wall angle. Block

gutter outlet with an old rag before removing mortar flashing, to keep out debris.

WHAT'S BEHIND YOUR WALLS?

All homes consist of a network of wires, pipes and cables, mostly hidden in the walls or under the floors. If you are pulling down walls, knocking in nails and so on, always check there is no danger of damaging any cables and pipes, to avoid the risk of water/gas leaks and electrocution.

ELECTRICITY

★ If you are hammering into walls and you're not sure where the wiring runs, turn the electricity off at the mains.

★ Establish where the main fuse box and meter is. Electricity comes into your home to the 'service head' – a sealed unit (which you are not allowed to interfere with) containing the main fuse that protects the whole system. From there single core cables run to your meter. You should be able to tell where the cables run by the positioning of your meter and of the various electrical sockets. This is usually behind the wainscot near the floor and running from socket to socket.

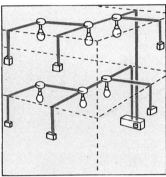

Wiring for lights usually runs behind the ceiling and from there down or along to the light fittings.

★ Take extra care if there has been a separate cable put in later – to a cooker for example – especially if it wasn't laid by a professional.

Equally, if you arrive in a new home and find light wires sticking out of the walls, they may still be live so don't start pulling them out or fixing new light fittings until you have turned the power off at the mains.

GAS PIPES

Gas comes into your home through large pipes. From the meter it may be carried to the boiler, fire, cooker and so on, through smaller pipes

WHAT'S BEHIND YOUR WALLS?

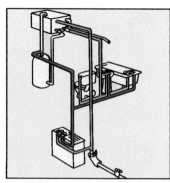

which probably run under the floorboards.
★ If lifting or hammering floorboards, always tackle them with caution. Don't hammer large nails into them without first lifting at least one to find out where the pipes may be running.

WATER PIPES

Although actual layout does vary from home to home, most domestic plumbing systems work in the same way and run along similar routes. The plumbing system consists of a network of pipes which carry hot and cold water around your home and also separate pipes for the central heating system.
★ Check where the tank is and trace the path of the pipes to the bathroom, toilet, outside tap and so on.
★ Check where the boiler is and trace the pipes to and from all the radiators – they usually run under the floorboards.
★ In older homes, especially converted ones, there may be mysterious pipes running up through ceilings into flats above. If in doubt, call a plumber to help discover what is connected to what.
★ Get to know where the stop cocks and valves are in case of emergencies.

NOTE: An underground service pipe runs from the water main into each building. Somewhere along this pipe is the water authority's stop cock. All water pipes and stop cocks your side of this are your responsibility. Find out where they are before you move into your home and before you are faced with an emergency. There should be a stop cock near the entry point of the supply to the house, another near the cold water cistern and another near the hot water cylinder. If there isn't, it may be worth installing them.

FITTING WINDOW LOCKS

Most locks come in two parts, one to fit to the opening part and the other to fit the frame. Which sort you choose depends on what your windows are made of and how they open and close. Also consider what sort of locking mechanism you want – some are quicker to lock and unlock than others.

CHOOSING THE LOCK

★ Most locks are easy to fit to wooden frames and some are also suitable for metal frames, if you use self-tapping screws designed for screwing into metal.

★ Some locks are specially designed for metal-frames.

★ Multi-purpose locks suit most windows while some toggle and snaplocks only suit casement windows. Use window bolts too for sash or casement windows.

★ All these locks can be seen from outside – an added deterrent. To keep sash windows looking neat you can buy screw bolts which fit inside the window frames.

FITTING THE LOCK

1 Choose a place on the opposite side to the hinges at a distance from the

FITTING WINDOW LOCKS

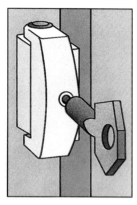

the type of lock which is best suited to your needs and requirements. Keep the keys handy, but somewhere they are not visible from outside. However, make sure that they are easily accessible in an emergency.

DOUBLE-GLAZED WINDOWS

Replacement double-glazed windows often have locks already fitted.

If you want to add extra locks you need to choose a sort that suits the material of the new frame. It's best to check with the window supplier which locks you should fit.

PATIO DOOR LOCKS

If you want to fit extra security devices in addition to existing locks, these should be screwed to the vertical part of the door frame, near the base. They have a bolt which fits into a hole drilled in the sliding panel to guard against the door being lifted out of the frame.

1 Mark out and drill pilot holes for self-tapping screws in the frame.

2 Start drilling a pilot hole for the large hole then slowly open it up to the required size.

existing window catches.

2 Position the lock and mark the screw holes on the window and frame.

3 Make pilot holes with a bradawl or drill, taking care not to go right through to the glass.

4 Drive in the screws.

Note: Some window bolts may need a recess chiselled out of the frame to allow the receiving plate to be fitted flush with the surface.

HOW THEY WORK

Some locks lock automatically when you close the window, or can be locked by the press of a button. Sash bolts, fitted inside window frames, can be fiddly and may take longer to lock and unlock than some other types. Choose

PERSONAL FILE

Use this card to keep a note of account numbers, customer reference numbers and any others you may need to refer to in order to deal with queries.

Gas Account No_____

Electricity Account No_____

Telephone Account No_____

Household contents insurance Policy No_____

Building insurance Policy No_____

Building society Account No_____

Water authority customer reference No_____

Community charge reference No_____

CAR

Insurance Policy No_____

Insurance due for renewal (date)_____

MOT due (date)_____

Road tax due (date)_____

PERSONAL FILE

Make a note of the serial numbers of your possessions so that, in case of burglary, you can help the police track them down. Take photos of valuables for easy identification.

Television_____

Video_____

Hi-fi system_____

CD player_____

Radio/cassette player_____

Microwave_____

Camera_____

Camera lenses_____

_____

_____

_____

_____

_____

_____

MORTGAGE FACT FILE

Keep a note of your mortgage arrangements so that you can check payment details at a glance and have all the information handy in case of enquiries.

Name of bank/building society ....

Branch address ....

Branch Tel No ....

Head office address ....

Head office Tel No ....

Mortgage Account No ....

Name of contact/broker for enquiries ....

Amount borrowed: £ ....

Date mortgage taken out ....

Term of mortgage .... years ....

Date due to end ....

Payment due on .... day of each month ....

Policy No of any relevant insurance policy ....

Name of insurance company/broker ....

Name of contact for enquiries ....

Address ....

Tel No ....

Amount of monthly insurance premium £ ....

MORTGAGE FACT FILE

Use this side of the card to record your current
monthly repayment and the date it came into effect.
This way you can keep track of its ups and downs and
make a note of the date on which you instructed any
necessary changes in standing orders etc.

Current monthly repayment	Payable from (date)	Date arranged
£..........................	....	....
£..........................	....	....
£..........................	....	....
£..........................	....	....
£..........................	....	....
£..........................	....	....
£..........................	....	....
£..........................	....	....
£..........................	....	....
£..........................	....	....
£..........................	....	....
£..........................	....	....
£..........................	....	....
£..........................	....	....
£..........................	....	....
£..........................	....	....
£..........................	....	....

FIRST-AID KITS

THE HOME KIT

★ Whether you're buying a ready-made kit or compiling your own, choose a sturdy, waterproof box with plenty of room inside for the contents listed below.

★ Make sure that the box is clearly marked and that all the members of your family know where to find it in an emergency.

★ Restock your first-aid kit after each item is used.

★ Make a list of useful telephone numbers (your doctor and the emergency department of your local hospital) and stick it inside the lid of the box.

★ This kit is an emergency kit only – intended to provide first aid until you can get professional help.

CONTENTS

Most of these items are easily obtained from chemists. If you have any problems finding the right size dressings, for example – ask your chemist to order them for you.

★ Box of 20 assorted, stretch fabric plasters. People allergic to the adhesive on fabric plasters may prefer the waterproof type.
Use these to cover small cuts and grazes.

★ Six antiseptic wipes.
Use to clean the skin.

★ One crêpe bandage (7.5cm x 4.5 metres).
Use to support a wrist or ankle joint or to keep non-adhesive dressings in place.

★ One roll adhesive fabric strip tape (3.8cm x 1 metre).
Use to keep non-adhesive dressings in place. The type that tears without scissors is especially useful in an emergency.

★ Primapore dressing pads – two 8.3cm x 6cm and two 12cm x 8.25cm.
Primapore dressings are absorbent, but allow the skin to breathe. They have a sticky backing and should be used to cover larger cuts and grazes.

★ Two medium and one large Propax sterile dressing pads.
Apply the appropriate size to a wound where some padding and support is needed.

★ One sterile, disposable triangular bandage.
Use as a sling to support an injured arm, or as a bandage (folded lengthways).

★ One glass thermometer in a case.
Take babies' and young children's temperatures by placing under the armpit, leaving at least five minutes before reading. For older

FIRST-AID KITS

children and adults, place under the tongue and leave at least two minutes before reading. If temperature is greater than 37.5°C, contact your doctor.

★ Safety pins.
Use to secure bandages or slings. Keep fastened when not in use.

★ Dressing scissors.
Use to cut dressings to size. Keep clean at all times.

★ Sharp-ended tweezers.
However, you should never attempt to deal with deeply embedded irritants yourself.

★ First-aid leaflet.

TRAVEL KIT
Emergencies away from home should always be dealt with by a professional – but having a basic first-aid kit in the car may come in handy for minor camping and day-trip accidents.

★ Box of waterproof plasters.
★ Six antiseptic wipes.
★ Crêpe bandage.
★ Fabric strip.
★ One pack Primapore pads.
★ One large pack Propax pads.
★ Safety pins.
★ Thermometer.
★ Scissors.
★ Tweezers (invaluable for splinters, but don't be tempted to deal with deeply embedded irritants – you should seek professional advice).

Travel sickness pills and personal medication should be kept out of the reach of children at all times, so only add them to your first-aid box if you can be sure they won't be tampered with.

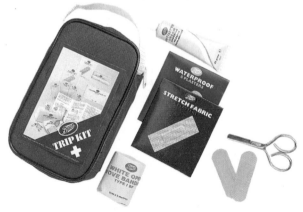

HOUSEHOLD ADHESIVES

Most household repairs can be achieved with one of the range of adhesives available at DIY shops and stores. If you're joining two surfaces made of different substances, remember that the more similar in structure the two surfaces, the stronger the bond will be. Always make sure both surfaces are clean and dry and follow manufacturers' instructions.

ALL-PURPOSE GLUE

(eg Evo-Stik Clear) Comes ready-mixed in a tube . Good for sticking card, paper and leather. Not very strong but easy to easy. Can be dissolved by nail varnish remover.

SUPER GLUE

(eg Loctite Super Glue 3) Comes ready-mixed in a non-clogging bottle or pen . Ideal for repairs to decorative pottery as it leaves no 'glue line'. Note: Not suitable for use on wine glasses or crockery that will be regularly submerged in warm, soapy water. Dissolve using washing-up liquid and hot water.

CONTACT ADHESIVE

(eg Bostik Contact) Needs to be applied thoroughly to both surfaces and left to become tacky before sticking. For use on plastic sheet materials and laminates. Some stick on impact; others allow you to slide the materials into place. Dissolve with special solvent designed for the purpose.

PVC CEMENT

(eg Loctite Vinyl Bond) Note: Very soft materials like polythene cannot be glued — if in doubt, try a little on an offcut first. For PVC and soft vinyl. Glue a patch of similar material over the back of the tear for a strong repair. Dissolve with a tiny amount of nail varnish remover. Use with care, as PVC and vinyl may 'melt' on contact.

HOUSEHOLD ADHESIVES

POLYSTYRENE CEMENT

(eg Bison Hard Plastics Adhesive) Works by melting and fusing the broken pieces together.

The sort of hard plastics used to make kitchen tools and kids' toys. Check the back of the pack for instructions on how to dissolve excess glue.

SYNTHETIC-LATEX GLUE

(eg Humbrol Ceiling Tile Adhesive) Is thick enough to fill quite large holes and cracks.

This is the glue to use when you want to attach polystyrene tiles and boards to walls and ceilings, whether for decoration or insulation. Remove excess glue with cold water.

RUBBER-RESIN/ LATEX GLUE

(eg Evo-Stik Flooring Adhesive) Sold in a tub and applied using a notched spreader.

Used to fix a range of hard floor coverings like vinyl and cork. Remove excess glue with clean water.

EPOXY RESIN

(eg Araldite) Sold in two parts – a hardener and a resin – which you mix together and then apply to both surfaces).

For achieving strong joints between small pieces of metal. Can also be used to repair plastics and ceramics where a neat finish is not vital. The resulting joint should be completely waterproof. Dissolve using methylated spirit.

ACRYLIC GLUE

(eg Bostik Hyperbond) Sold in two parts – each applied to one of the surfaces before they are joined.

Use for repairs to crockery. Does leave a glue line but this can be removed using a sharp knife once it has hardened.

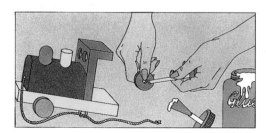

NB Act fast. Don't wait for the stain to dry.

Basic techniques

1 Flush out wet stains such as blood, juice, coffee or tea with cold water. Never use hot water. A little washing-up liquid may help remove the stain.

2 Absorb non-greasy stains such as wine or fruit juice with salt or tissues. Leave salt until it has absorbed the spilt liquid; press tissues onto the stain (don't rub).

3 Dissolve greasy stains with solvents such as proprietary spot removers, white spirit, surgical spirit or acetone.

As a last resort: try bleach to get out any residual stain. Bleaches include hydrogen peroxide applied with a medicine dropper. Put a pad of tissue under the stain. (Don't pour any peroxide back into the bottle.) Dygon will remove many tea, coffee, wine, fruit and other non-greasy stains **from white fabric only.**

DOs and DONT's

DO read the care label.

DO air fabrics after using chemical stain removers.

DO test delicate fabrics first.

DON'T rub wool while it's wet.

DON'T use acetone on acetate fabrics.

DON'T use bleach on coloured fabrics.

INSTANT GUIDE TO COMMON STAINS

Alcohol: Flush red wine with white vinegar or white wine and rinse. Treat the residual stain with biological detergent; rinse well. Or try hydrogen peroxide diluted half and half with water. Rinse well. Wash at high temperature if fabric allows.

Blood: Flush or soak in cold salt water. Dried stains may respond to soaking in hydrogen peroxide solution (test fabric first).

Butter, cream and fat: Scrape with blunt knife. Wash at

high temperature or dissolve with a solvent, then wash. Use absorbent if the fabric is particularly delicate.

Candle wax: Scrape with blunt knife. Sandwich fabric between sheets of kitchen tissue and melt wax with warm iron on lowest setting. Dissolve any residue with solvent. Treat remaining colour with white spirit and rinse well.

Chocolate and cocoa: Scrape off with blunt knife. Flush with cold water. Treat with liquid detergent. Mop with tissue, rinse, and use solvent for any residual stain.

Coffee and tea: Soak in cold or hand-hot washing detergent solution and rinse well. Treat residual stains with hydrogen peroxide diluted half and half.

On carpets and rugs, squirt with a soda siphon (don't saturate fabric), then carpet shampoo. If persistent greasy cream or milk stains remain, sponge them with solvent.

Curry powder: Difficult to remove, especially from cotton. Soak in diluted household ammonia or white spirit. Or use bleach (make sure you test the fabric first).

Hot fat: Hot fat may fuse fibres together. Don't use dry-cleaning solvent, which may remove the colour. Treat with liquid detergent and repeat if necessary.

Fruit, fruit juices, soft drinks: Rinse with cold water, treat with liquid detergent, then rinse again. Treat residue with diluted household ammonia then diluted hydrogen peroxide; rinse again. Suitable fabrics should be washed in a hot wash.

Gravy: Flush with cold water or liquid detergent. Dry borax powder dissolved in the water may help and will not harm delicate fabrics.

Ketchup: Remove deposit, sponge with liquid detergent solution and rinse. Or use solvent. May need to be cleaned professionally.

Meat juices: Treat as for blood.

Oil: Dissolve with solvent; repeat several times. Soak the fabric, then treat with white spirit with a little white vinegar added. Rinse.

Sauce: Treat as for gravy.

MENDING CHINA

Using modern adhesives, broken china can be mended to look almost like new, but it is important to follow each stage of the procedure carefully and work slowly and patiently.

Collect all the tools and materials you will need before you start.

TOOLS

★ Foam rubber sponge, shaving brush and old toothbrush for cleaning broken edges.

★ Pipe cleaners for getting into nooks and crannies.

★ Small craft knife for scraping off old glue.

★ Magnifying glass.

★ Pieces of sticky paper, clamps and box of sand for holding bits together while the glue sets.

Note: Breaks should be repaired as soon as possible, before dirt has settled on the broken edges. If this is not practical, keep all the pieces in a sealed plastic bag until they can be mended.

ADHESIVES

★ For everyday china use an **epoxy** adhesive. These come in quick- or slow-drying forms. Once set, it's stuck for good.

★ To practise, or for very special china, on display only, use a **china cement**, or a **household glue**, which can be unstuck again if necessary.

★ **Acrylic** or **cyanoacrylate adhesives** are suitable for valuable china or glass, because they can be dissolved and the piece taken apart again. Won't stand up to washing, though.

WORKING TIPS

★ Wipe the broken edges with a piece of silk or other non-fluffy cloth. If the break is old, wash in diluted washing-up liquid. If mended before, place in a solution of detergent and bring to the boil (or rub with acetone on a clean silk cloth).

★ Don't boil cracked china to dissolve old glue.

★ Don't touch broken edges with fingers, as the glue won't adhere to greasy surfaces.

★ Work with warm hands.

★ Use as little glue as possible

MENDING CHINA

and follow manufacturers' instructions.

GLUING
1. Lay the pieces on a table in the order you want to put them together.
2. Fit the pieces together dry to make sure they match up.
3. Glue the edges of two pieces and stick them together carefully. Allow each join to set slightly before attaching any more pieces.
4. Remove surplus adhesive from the joins as you fit each piece according to the manufacturer's instructions. You may need to use the point of a knife.

CLAMPING
1. Use masking tape or lick-and-stick brown paper tape for holding pieces in position while they set.
2. Tack nails onto a board

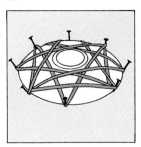

around the mended plate and stretch rubber bands between them to hold it flat.
3. A box full of sand can be used to hold the china.

FILLING
Using epoxy putty:
1. Press the putty well into the crack with a knife blade.
2. Leave the filling slightly proud of the object.
3. When hardened, rub the putty down with first-grade wet-and-dry paper.
4. Paint over repair if necessary, and varnish.

QUICK CONVERSION

TEMPERATURES
★ To convert Fahrenheit to centigrade, subtract 32 and multiply by 0.5555.
★ To convert centigrade to Fahrenheit, multiply by 1.8 and add 32.

CENTIGRADE/CELSIUS

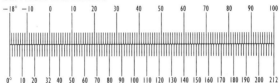

FAHRENHEIT

FABRIC WIDTHS
Fabric widths are sold by the metre in standard widths of:

90cm (36in)	140cm (55in)
115cm (45in)	150cm (60in)

LENGTHS
★ To convert feet to centimetres multiply by 30.48.
★ To convert centimetres to feet divide by 30.48.
★ To convert yards to metres multiply by 0.9144.
★ To convert metres to yards divide by 0.9144.

OVEN TEMPERATURES

ELECTRIC		GAS	SOLID FUEL
°C	°F		
70	150		
80	175		
100	200	Low	
110	225	¼	
120	250	½	Very cool
140	275	1	Cool
150	300	2	
160	325	3	Slow
180	350	4	Moderate
190	375	5	
200	400	6	Moderately hot
220	425	7	Hot
230	450	8	Very hot
240	475	9	Very hot

Figures on tables have been rounded up slightly to make them easier to compare.

METRIC																
5mm	1cm	2.5cm	5cm	7cm	10cm	12cm	15cm	18cm	20cm	13cm	25cm	28cm	30cm	91cm	1m	3.05m
IMPERIAL																
¼in	½in	1in	2in	3in	4in	5in	6in	7in	8in	9in	10in	11in	12in (1ft)	36in	39in	10ft

QUICK CONVERSION

WEIGHTS
★ To convert pounds to kilograms multiply by 0.4536.
★ To convert kilograms to pounds divide by 0.4536.
★ To convert ounces to grams multiply by 28.3495.
★ To convert grams to ounces divide by 28.3495.

LIQUIDS
★ To convert UK pints to litres multiply by 0.568.
★ To convert USA pints to litres multiply by 0.473.
★ To convert litres to UK pints divide by 0.568.
★ To convert litres to USA pints divide by 0.473.

METRIC	IMPERIAL
5g	¼oz
15g	½oz
25g	1oz
50g	2oz
85g	3oz
110g	4oz
140g	5oz
180g	6oz
200g	7oz
225g	8oz
250g	9oz
280g	10oz
300g	11oz
340g	12oz
375g	13oz
400g	14oz
425g	15oz
450g	16oz (1lb)
1 kilogram	2·2lb

METRIC	IMPERIAL	USA
5ml	⅛fl oz	1 tsp
15ml	½fl oz	1 tbsp
25ml	1fl oz	⅛ cup
50ml	2fl oz	¼ cup
65ml	2½fl oz	⅓ cup
100ml	4fl oz	½ cup
150ml	5fl oz	⅔ cup
175ml	6fl oz	¾ cup
225ml	8fl oz	1 cup (½ USA pt)
300ml	10fl oz (½ UK pt)	1¼ cups
350ml	12fl oz	1½ cups
400ml	14fl oz	1¾ cups
475ml	16fl oz	2 cups (1 USA pt)
600ml	20fl oz (1 UK pt)	2½ cups
750ml	24fl oz	3 cups
900ml	32fl oz	4 cups (2 USA pt)
1 litre	35fl oz	4¼ cups
1.14 litres	40fl oz (2 UK pt)	5 cups

ASSOCIATIONS AND WATCH-DOGS

Do you know which organisations to turn to for help and advice? Listed below are a few associations and 'watch dogs' with the consumers' interests at heart...

British Association of Removal Firms
3 Churchill Court,
58 Station Road,
North Harrow HA2 7SA
(081-861 3331)
Investigates removal companies before allowing them to become association members. Tries to reconcile complaints about their members from dissatisfied customers. Will also give advice on pursuing complaints about non-member companies. Provides names of removal companies in its membership (please supply an sae).

Building Employers Confederation
82 New Cavendish Street,
London WIM 8AD
(071-580 5588)
Trade association with its own code of practice (no building codes of practice have Office of Fair Trading approval, however). Will check that builders employed by consumers are members of their confederation and also offer a guarantee scheme on building work.

Citizens Advice Bureaux (CAB) Your local CAB office is listed in the phone book. Provides free, confidential and impartial advice and information to anyone on any subject. Particularly helpful in circumstances where referrals or advice on unfair treatment are required.

Consumers' Association
2 Marylebone Road,
London NWI 4DX
(071-486 5544)
Campaigns for improvements in goods and services and tests everything from vacuum cleaners to house paint on the consumer's behalf. Research results are published in *Which?* magazines on health, gardening, holidays and a series of useful self-help books.

Gas Consumers Council
6th Floor, Abford House,
15 Wilton Road,
London SWIV ILT
(071-931 0977)
Represents the interests of consumers in the 12 regions of British Gas. The council will deal with complaints from individuals who have been unable to

ASSOCIATIONS AND WATCH-DOGS

resolve matters with their own gas regions.

Glass and Glazing Federation
44 Borough High Street,
London SE1 1XB
(071-403 7177)
Supplies a code of practice and arbitration scheme, which is recognised by the Office of Fair Trading and can be used by dissatisfied consumers against member companies (as long as they are still trading). This trade association also supplies a list of its members. Phone for regional information.

Office of Fair Trading
Field House,
15/25 Bream's Buildings,
London EC4A 1PR
(071-242 2858)
Protects consumers by ensuring that trade practices are as fair as possible. Works closely with the Department of Trade and Industry and with local authority trading standards departments. Also provides consumer packs and information on home improvements, credit agencies, consumer rights etc.

The Office of Telecommunications (OFTEL) Export House,
50 Ludgate Hill,
London EC4M 7JJ
(071-822 1600)
Deals with consumer complaints about telephone services and is also the industry watchdog. Will take up complaints about Mercury as well as British Telecom. It also has two specialist committees which handle complaints on behalf of elderly and disabled users.

Post Office Users' National Council (POUNC)
Waterloo Bridge House,
Waterloo Road,
London SE1 8UA
(071-928 9458)
Takes up complaints and makes representations about postal services. Also examines proposals for tariff and policy changes put forward by the Post Office. There are separate User Councils for Scotland and Wales (see below).

Post Office Users' Council For Scotland 43 Jeffrey Street, Edinburgh EH1 1DN
(031-2445576)

Post Office Users' Council For Wales Caradog House,
1/6 St Andrews Place,
Cardiff CF1 3BE
(0222 374028)

BUGS AND PESTS

SAFETY RULES
★ Keep all surfaces clean.
★ Make sure food is covered.
★ Fill cracks in floorboards and walls, and block up holes behind skirtings and under the kitchen sink.
★ Disinfect the rubbish bin regularly and keep it covered.
★ Tie or seal rubbish bags before putting them outside.
★ Remember that insecticides can be harmful to humans and their pets so always follow manufacturers' instructions.

REMEMBER
If you have a serious infestation, call in the local health authority.

DEALING WITH COMMON PESTS
Ants: are fairly harmless, but cause a nuisance when they come into the house.
★ Follow them to find out where they are entering the house and block their way with a piece of cotton wool soaked in paraffin.
★ If you can discover the nest, destroy it with a suitable pesticide.
Cockroaches: will lurk in inaccessible places, behind the fridge for example, and eat food, fabrics and paper.
★ Sprinkle likely areas daily with pyrethrum powder or an insecticide powder until the

cockroaches have gone.
Flies: breed in rubbish, especially in hot weather.
★ Use dustbin liners and seal them when full.
★ Use spray insecticides with great care and cover all food before using a spray.
★ Slow-release vaporised killers should last six months, but do not use in small rooms.
Mice: will eat food and cause damage in the house.
★ Use a trap (several 'humane' designs are now available). Peanut butter, bacon and cake are good baits.
★ Anticoagulant poisons can be used, but other poisons are highly dangerous and should only be used by professionals.
★ Block up holes, especially in cupboards or under the sink.
Rats: carry some particularly nasty diseases – if you have an infestation you should call in your local health authority.
★ Don't leave old cardboard

BUGS AND PESTS

boxes or rags lying around for rats to make nests in.

Silver-fish: like damp, cool places. They can damage books and fabrics.

★ Use household insecticides on doors, windows, skirtings, cupboards and pipework.

Wasps, bees and hornets:

★ Get the local authority to deal with nests.

Fleas: in an animal may lead to dermatitis, tapeworm or allergies. Animal fleas will bite humans.

★ De-flea pets regularly and protect them by using anti-flea grooming brushes, collars and discs. Do not use cat products on dogs or vice versa.

★ Use disposable bedding for pets and change it frequently.

★ In cool temperatures flea eggs can remain dormant for over two months so vacuum regularly and burn the contents of the bag.

★ Apply a suitable insecticide to furniture.

Mosquitoes: are found near stagnant water butts, puddles and ponds.

★ Pyrethrum is a suitable insecticide and won't harm fish or plants when sprayed in ponds.

★ Mosquito-repellent rings can be used. Often made of pyrethrum, they burn down slowly and should be used with the windows closed.

IRONING GUIDE

SAFETY

● When buying an iron, make sure the label confirms that it meets the safety standards of its country of manufacture.
● Never fill a steam iron while it is switched on.
● Never let small children near the iron while in use.
● Always switch the iron off if you leave it to answer the telephone etc.
● Let the iron cool down before you wind the cord around it for storage.

MAINTENANCE

● If your iron takes distilled water you can use defrosted water from your fridge.

● Clean non-stick sole plates with a weak solution of warm water and detergent.
● To remove persistent stains, use very fine wire wool WHEN THE IRON IS COLD.

HOT TIPS

● Start with cool-iron items and raise the temperature as you get to more robust fabrics.
● Leave the iron on for five minutes before ironing until the thermostat settles down.

● If your iron is non-steam, iron while clothes are damp. If they have dried, spray with water and roll up to spread the dampness before you begin.
● If using steam, always keep the iron at the steam setting.

TROUSERS

1 Turn the trousers inside out and iron the pockets flat.
2 Turn back to right side. Fit the waist over the board and iron the tops and waistband.
3 Fold lengthways, seams down centre. Iron inside and outside of each leg. (If you don't want creases, stop short of the edge.)

IRONING GUIDE

SHIRTS AND DRESSES
1 Start at the top of the garment and work down.
2 Iron the collar on both sides, starting at the points and working in towards the centre back.
3 Iron the cuffs on both sides.
4 Iron the sleeves, starting at the under-arm seams.
5 Iron the body, starting at one front and working round across the back to the other.
6 Hang the garment up to air before folding.

PROFESSIONAL FINISH
● **Teatowels, pillow-cases etc:** Pull them into shape before ironing.
● **Pleats:** Tack into place before ironing.
● **Sheets:** Fold beforehand, turning and refolding as you iron until all surfaces are smooth.
● **Embossed cottons:** Press gently on the **wrong** side, instead of sliding the iron.
● **Acetate, acrylic, crêpe, cotton lace, linen, silk, triacetate, matt viscose, Viyella and wool:** Iron inside out while damp.
● **Cotton, net, silky viscose:** Iron on the right side.

PRESSING
Use this technique for fabrics that should not have the iron placed directly on them (such as tweeds and fabrics that become shiny when ironed).
1 Use a hot iron and a clean, damp teatowel.
2 Place garment on the ironing board with the teatowel on top.
3 Press the iron down, then lift, then press down again, until the fabric underneath is smooth. Move cloth to a new position and continue over entire surface, re-dampening the cloth as necessary.
NOTE: Air garments thoroughly after pressing.

STORING CLOTHES

FIRST PRINCIPLES

1 Wash or dry-clean all items to be stored.

2 Mend all tears and replace all buttons.

3 Air garments thoroughly after ironing and before folding.

4 Do not pack garments too tightly as it will damage fibres.

5 Do not starch items before storing them.

MOTHPROOFING

★ Moths like natural fibres (wool, linen, cotton and silk). Protect them with a proprietary product from hardware stores, available in sachet or spray form.

★ Clothes stored in polythene are usually safe from moths.

★ Lavender and wormwood (Artemisia) make good natural moth repellants.

WHERE TO STORE

Flat storage

★ Store knitted and jersey clothes flat.

★ Large laundry hampers, trunks, blanket chests or chests-of-drawers all make useful flat storage.

★ All should be lined with wallpaper or plastic.

★ Don't squash items or you will damage the fibres.

Hanging space

★ Hang ties over expanded curtain wire, fixed flat inside wardrobe.

★ Hang belts by buckles from hooks fixed to wardrobe.

★ Hangers should be padded.

★ Hang shirts if you have enough cupboard space.

★ Do not hang clothes from the loop at the neck.

★ Cover delicate garments with special plastic covers (or dustbin bags).

Hats

★ Store in boxes, lightly padded with tissue.

★ Don't store with crown against flat surface.

STORING CLOTHES

Shirts and dresses
1 Place white tissue paper between the folds to prevent harsh creases.

2 Lie garment face down. Fold one side plus arm to middle; fold back down on itself; repeat with other side; take top down to bottom, keeping sleeves inside.

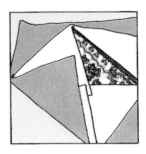

Trousers and suits
★ Fold trousers along crease and store on hanger. Tape folded card or foam rubber along cross bar of hanger.

Pleated skirts
★ Fold or roll the skirt carefully, in the direction of the pleats. Cut the foot off an old stocking, draw skirt through and store flat in the stocking.

Delicate fabrics
★ Lace and silk should be completely wrapped, first in white and then in blue tissue paper (white won't mark fabric, blue keeps out light). Don't fold too tightly.
★ Beat fur gently, then shake well before storing.

Footwear
★ Support with shoe-trees or rolled-up newspaper.
★ Wrap in plastic carrier bags and store at the bottom of a chest or hamper.

HOME LAUNDRY

Always follow the washing instructions on fabric care labels.

⭐ Wash clothes at the recommended temperature – fabrics washed at too low a temperature will not clean effectively, and too high a temperature can cause damage.

⭐ If your washing load is made up of garments with different fibre contents, select the gentlest and lowest temperature wash indicated on any of the garment labels.

⭐ Mixed-fibre fabrics should be washed at the temperature recommended for more delicate yarns.

⭐ Don't put deep-dye fabrics into a mixed load until you're sure that they won't run. Wash separately until they become colour-safe!

⭐ Flame-retardant fabrics should not be washed above 50°C. Check labels for correct washing solution. Soap can damage flame-retardant finishes – some detergents may be recommended instead.

⭐ Fibre contents have to appear, by law, on household fabric and clothing labels. If only one kind of fibre has been used, just the name may be given. For example, 'Wool', possibly preceded by '100 per cent' or 'all pure'.

⭐ Pure wool garments carrying the relevant wash-care label can be washed safely in a warm cycle (40°C) and spun on a gentle spin-cycle.

⭐ Protect the outer surfaces of wool garments by turning them inside out before washing.

⭐ Do not tumble-dry wool garments.

These five basic symbols appear (in various combinations) on fabric care labels:

 Bleaching

 Washing

 Tumble-drying

 Ironing

 May be dry-cleaned

⭐ A cross through any of these symbols means DO NOT (bleach, tumble-dry, wash etc).

⭐ One dot shown inside the

53

tumble-dry symbol indicates a low heat setting. Two dots indicate a high heat setting.

WASHING MACHINE SYMBOLS

The 'wash tub' symbol indicates normal washing action. The number shown on the tub is the recommended water temperature in degrees Celsius.

The bar underneath the symbol indicates a reduced washing action – wash as for synthetic fibres.

A broken bar means wash gently. Reduce the machine action by selecting a setting you'd use for wool.

★ If you're in any doubt about the machine setting required for different fabrics, check the textile machine codes shown on washing powder or detergent packs.

BLEACHING

★ Chlorine bleach will whiten pure cotton or linen fabrics, but should not be used on mixed-fibre fabrics. A 'greener' solution is to use non-chlorine bleach on any bleachable garments.

Chlorine bleach may be used

Do not bleach

DRYING

★ The heat from a tumble-drier can damage fibres, causing them to shrink. Check fabric care labels and if in any doubt, hang garments out on the line.

★ Woollens and delicate fibres should be coaxed gently back into shape while still damp and then dried flat.

★ Never dry wool items in front of an open gas or electric fire and don't tumble-dry unless the wash-care label says that you can.

★ Delicate, light-coloured fibres can discolour if dried in strong summer daylight or direct sunshine.

★ When using a hanger for drip-dry clothes, check that the weight of the garment will not pull down on the hanger and stretch the fabric out of shape.

DRAUGHTPROOFING

If you added up all the gaps between doors and windows and their frames, the hole would measure 1.2sq m (12.9sq ft) in the average house – plenty of room for heat to escape through! Draught-proofing is cheap, quick and easy and you will begin saving on fuel bills immediately.

WINDOWS AND DOORS

Sticky tape: Some windows can be kept closed all winter. Masking tape across the gaps will keep out draughts but it is not always easy to remove in spring, so don't use it unless you intend to redecorate then.

Foam strip: Adhesive foam strip can be fixed to the frame (right). This retracts when the window is closed, sealing gaps. It sticks to metal and wood and is invisible when windows are closed. It will not fill large gaps. Replace every two years.

● The frame should be dry and clean before applying.

Other types of interior draught excluder include **Plastic Strip** (a flexible tube which is squashed when the door closes to seal the gap), **V-shaped strips** and strips with **sprung, hinged flaps** in bronze, copper or plastic.

● Metal strips have a long life; plastic is cheaper and more flexible (good for crooked houses) but lasts only about three years.

● Read instructions and fix with care.

EXTERNAL DOORS

Easiest and cheapest is a plain strip of wood or plastic with an edge of bristles or rubber which brushes against the floor (below). For badly fitting doors, use an aluminium strip holding a plastic tube which compresses to form a seal.

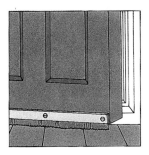

DRAUGHTPROOFING

FIREPLACES
Block off completely if not in use. Fix chipboard, plywood or cardboard cut to exact size over gap.

SKIRTINGS AND FLOORS
● Fill gaps between boards with papier mâché, bad gaps with slivers of wood fixed with wood glue.
● Carpet will help to eliminate any draughts.
● Nail strips of quadrant moulding where the skirting meets the floor and paint to match the skirting.

LETTER BOXES
Fix a close-fitting flap to the inner side so the flap swings inwards only, or fix a large box that covers the opening to inside of door to hold letters.

CAT FLAPS
Choose one that closes tightly – you can now get lockable flaps.

ABC OF HOUSEHOLD CHEMICALS

A guide to common household cleaners and their properties.

ACETONE: Solvent for animal and vegetable oils. Will dissolve acetate. Flammable.

AMMONIA: Alkali with pungent odour used in many cleaners. Don't inhale fumes.

AMYL ACETATE: Solvent for cellulose paint and adhesives. Highly flammable and toxic.

BATHROOM AND KITCHEN CLEANERS: Cream cleaners, abrasive powder cleaners and liquid cleaners use various combinations of chemicals, including ammonia, chlorine, ethanol, formaldehyde. Toxic.

BLEACHES: Most household bleaches contain **sodium hypochlorite. Hydrogen peroxide** is milder. Use **sodium perborate** on silk or wool or sodium hydrosulphite on nylon and wool.

BORAX: Alkali mineral salt used as water softener for laundry and antiseptic in shampoos. Quite mild.

CAUSTIC SODA/LYE: (see **sodium hyroxide**).

DESCALING PRODUCTS: Most contain ammonia and caustic ingredients.

DISINFECTANTS: Many household disinfectants contain

poisonous and corrosive bleaches such as chlorine, phenol, chloroxylenol, or ammonium compounds which are non toxic but environmentally unfriendly.

FLUOROCARBONS: range of synthetic chemicals, some used as dry-cleaning solvents for delicate fabrics.

HYDROGEN PEROXIDE: Comparatively mild disinfectant and bleach.

INSECTICIDES AND PESTICIDES: Many contain organic chemicals toxic to humans which can accumulate in the body. Slow-release products contain a dangerous biocide which may be breathed or find its way onto food.

LAVATORY CLEANERS: Some contain strong alkali usually **sodium hydroxide** (caustic soda). Will burn through most substances. Never use two toilet

ABC OF HOUSEHOLD CHEMICALS

cleaners together – they
may be explosive and/or
toxic.

METHYLATED SPIRITS:
Ethanol with additives.
Dissolves essential oils, shellac,
some dyes, ball-point pen ink,
iodine, grass stains. Highly
flammable and poisonous.

OVEN CLEANERS: Caustic
cleaners strongly alkaline.

PARAFFIN: From petroleum.
Used in some furniture
polishes, cold creams, hair
preparations, as rust remover.
Poisonous and flammable.

SILICONES: Derived from
silica. Tough ingredient
used to help spread polishes.

SODIUM: Large family of
compound of sodium, many
used in the manufacture of
washing products.

Sodium bicarbonate (baking
powder) – used as mild alkali
for laundry-work.

Sodium carbonate (washing
soda) – alkali for laundry, water
softener, varnish remover,
drain cleaner. Don't use on
aluminium, silk, wool,
sisal, vinyl.

**Sodium
hexametaphosphate**
(Calgon) – water softener.
Neutral, gentler than washing
soda, dissolves easily.

Sodium hydroxide (caustic
soda/lye) – very strong alkali.

Used in loo and oven cleaners,
soap. Poisonous and caustic.

Sodium hypochlorite
(Javelle water) – household
bleach or chlorine bleach.

Sodium perborate – soft
bleach for all fabrics.

Sodium silicate (waterglass)
– egg preserver and paint
stain remover.

TRICHLOROETHANE:
Non-flammable solvent used in
household grease-stain
removers.

TURPENTINE: Derived
from pine trees. Solvent.

VINEGAR: Dilute, impure
acetic acid, made from beer,
weak wine etc. Many uses for
cleaning.

WASHING SODA: See
sodium.

WHITE SPIRIT: Colourless
solvent for use as paint
thinners, general-purpose
grease and stain remover.
Flammable and toxic.

CLEANING JEWELLERY

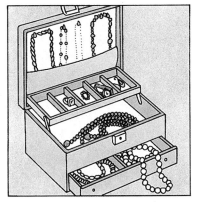

Keep all jewellery in separate boxes or compartments. If necessary wrap each piece in tissue or cotton wool. Bear in mind that gold and platinum are delicate and diamonds are particularly likely to damage other items.

In general, jewellery can be washed in **warm** water and mild detergent – using a soft toothbrush to get into the intricate parts. (Hot water might cause the setting to expand and allow the stones to drop out.)

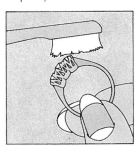

A little household ammonia in the water helps to loosen the dirt, but never use it on pearls.

Prevent tarnish on cheap costume jewellery by painting it with clear nail varnish.

Gold and platinum
★ Rub gently with a piece of chamois. Ordinary cloths can harbour grit.

Silver
Use a proprietary jewellery cleaner for silver with stones set in it.

Diamonds
★ Use a soft paintbrush to loosen any dirt at the back of the setting.
★ Boil diamonds for a few minutes in a weak solution of soapsuds and a few drops of ammonia. Allow the piece of jewellery to cool and then dip it in white spirit. Lay it on a bed

CLEANING JEWELLERY

of paper tissues to dry.
★ DO NOT boil diamond jewellery if there are other stones in the setting too.

Pearls and coral
★ Pearl necklaces should be re-strung whenever they become loose.
★ Clean by rubbing gently with a clean chamois. Work carefully between the beads.
★ Pearls on their own may be washed in warm water and mild detergent but don't wash necklaces in case the water rots the thread.
★ Wear your pearls frequently or they will lose their lustre.

Costume jewellery
★ Wash in warm water but don't soak. If stones become loose, use an epoxy resin to fix.

Acrylic jewellery
★ Sponge with lukewarm water and mild detergent. Wipe with clean damp cloth.
★ Clean any scratches with metal polish.

Wooden jewellery
★ Wipe with a damp cloth and finish with a little wax polish or olive oil.

Bead and stone necklaces
★ Clean stones and old beads

with dry baking soda sprinkled on a brush.
★ Re-string about once a year.

Amber
★ Wipe with warm soapy water and dry immediately. Buff with chamois leather.
★ Remove greasy marks with a bread ball or wipe over with a drop of almond oil.
★ DON'T treat amber jewellery with alcohol or any solvent because it will remove the shiny surface.

Opals
★ 'Dry wash' them by leaving them overnight in a jar of powdered magnesia. Remove the powder with a soft brush.
★ Opals can break easily, so don't subject them to extremes of temperature.

Ivory
★ Ivory should not be washed. It will stay whiter longer if stored in the light.
★ Rub with a soft cloth dipped in almond oil to give it a protective coating.
★ Old ivory should be cleaned professionally.
★ Bleach yellow ivory by rubbing it with a cloth dipped in 20vol hydrogen peroxide (available from chemists) and leave it in the sun to dry.

CLEANING GLASS

Cut glass
★ Bowls should be washed in warm water and washing-up liquid.
★ Use a soft brush to get into the crevices.

★ Put them on a cloth or piece of paper towel to drain.

Table tops, shelves and cupboard fronts
★ Rub with a cut lemon, or vinegar and water and dry with paper kitchen towels. Buff up with newspaper.
★ Alternatively, use a few drops of household ammonia in warm water or a proprietary window cleaner.
★ Scratched glass surfaces should be rubbed with chamois leather impregnated with jewellers' rouge, pressing lightly.

Decanters and vases
Decanters and vases with narrow necks are notoriously difficult to clean. There are various substances which, when shaken about in the decanter, will loosen flower and plant verdigris and wine sediment. All the following

★ After drying, polish with a silver cloth or stainless-steel cleaner.
★ Leave badly stained cut glass to soak for several hours in a warm solution of water, detergent and ammonia.

Table glass
★ When washing up, deal with the glasses first, when the water will be at its cleanest. Use a meagre squeeze of washing-up liquid and rinse in clear, hot water. Drain on a soft cloth.
★ Glasses with stems should be held by the stem.
★ Wash glass pieces one at a time, using a plastic bowl to prevent chipping.

CLEANING GLASS

methods are reliable and easy:
★ Shake tea leaves and vinegar in the vase.

★ Fill the vessel with water and 2 tsp of household ammonia and allow to stand overnight.
★ Roll small ball bearings around the base.
★ Fill the vessel with clean sand or aquarium gravel, add a squeeze of washing-up liquid and a little warm water and shake well. Use a bottle brush to clear out all the sediment completely.
★ Remove the whitish watermark on vases by rubbing a cut lemon around the line. Leave a few minutes if necessary and then wash as usual.
★ OR use a dentifrice powder solution of a heaped teaspoon in half a tumbler of water. Leave overnight then wash as usual.

Glass oven-to-tableware
★ Clean as for other pans: soak off burnt-on food; scour if necessary with a nylon or steel wool pad.
NOTE: Don't put a very cold pan straight onto a hot stove or a very hot one onto a cold surface. The sudden change in temperature may cause it to break.

Glass lampshades
★ Always turn the electricity off at the mains before cleaning any piece of electrical equipment.
★ Unscrew and wash occasionally in a mild water and detergent solution.
★ Kitchen lampshades tend to get dirtier than others so use a stronger detergent solution to clean them.
★ Dust chandeliers whenever you clean the room.
★ To wash chandeliers, wipe all the parts with a cloth wrung out in a water and detergent solution.

Light bulbs
★ Take light bulbs out of sockets about once a month and wipe with a damp cloth. Make sure the bulb is dry before putting it back.
★ Wipe fluorescent tubes with a damp cloth.

CLEANING LEATHER

Upholstery

Hide furniture can become dry and parched. In order to prevent this, you should do one of the following things at least once a year:

★ Dust carefully with a clean cloth, then apply a hide food or saddle soap sparingly with swabs of cotton wool, using as little water as possible. Leave for 24 hours and then polish with a soft, clean duster.

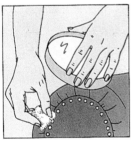

★ Sponge furniture with a solution of I tsp household ammonia and 4 tsp vinegar and 600ml (I pint) water. Then apply castor oil on a rag. When the leather is dry, polish with furniture cream.

★ Rub dark leather with castor oil to prevent cracking. On pale leather use petroleum jelly.

Desk tops

★ Wash with a barely damp cloth wrung out in a mild detergent solution.

★ Rub with leather renovator or hide food.

★ Rub ink stains very gently with cotton wool dipped in white spirit, but use sparingly because it can remove colour.

Note: Avoid touching any embossed gilding and the surrounding wood.

Tips for particular leathers

Buckskin: Brush well. Use sandpaper for difficult marks or use a proprietary cleaner.

Calf: If dried too quickly, calf can become stiff. Soften it by rubbing a mixture of milk and water into the surface.

Crocodile: Buff with a soft cloth after use and use shoe cream occasionally.

Pigskin: Very difficult to clean. Try dry-cleaning powder such as fuller's earth to absorb grease, then remove gently with a soft brush.

Suede: Clean regularly.

★ Remove oil and grease stains

CLEANING LEATHER

with a thick paste of fuller's earth and a little dry cleaning fluid. Rub into the stain. Leave for several hours then brush off. DON'T use a chemical fluid or spot cleaner on its own – it will leave an ugly ring.

★ Use a special suede cleaning cloth to brush dirty marks from the neck.

★ Brush suede in a circular motion with a soft rubber or bristle brush or a special wire suede brush. Perk up 'tired' suede with proprietary suede cleaner.

★ Protect **clean** suede with a proprietary stain repellent.

★ To revive 'flattened' suede, hold the article over a boiling kettle spout and allow the steam to get well into the nap.

Buff up with a soft-bristle brush.

Fake leathers

★ Wipe sticky marks with a cloth squeezed in a warm detergent solution (not soap)

and polish with a duster.

★ DON'T use wax or cream polishes because they tend to leave the surface sticky.

Boots, shoes and bags

★ Remove dried mud with a stiff brush.

★ Apply cream or polish and buff with a soft brush or cloth.

★ Use a small velvet pad or 'buffer' for a brilliant shine.

★ Clean patent leather with a soft, damp cloth and detergent. Wax will crack the leather. Alternatively, use a half-and-half mix of lanolin and castor oil. Buff up with a soft cloth.

Leather gloves

★ Wash gloves on your hands in warm water and soap flakes. Leave some of the soap in the gloves after washing. Dry them over a wooden or wire hand, or pull them into shape and hang them over bottles to let the air in. When dry, rub the leather between your fingers to soften it.

CLEANING SILVER/METALS

When using proprietary products make sure you use the right product for the metal. In many cases there are simpler 'natural' substances you can use instead. Always wear cotton gloves or the acids from your skin will tarnish the metal.

Don't attempt to clean valuable antiques yourself – you could do irreparable damage. They should be cleaned professionally.

SILVER AND SILVER PLATE

Silver needs constant care because it can tarnish very quickly. To prevent tarnishing:

★ Wash in hot water and detergent immediately after use. Rinse and dry at once.

★ Don't wrap silver in plastic and don't use elastic bands to secure wrappings. (Acid-free tissue papers, protective bags, and cloth impregnated with tarnish inhibitors are all available from jewellers.)

Cleaning tips

★ Rub tarnished silver with a proprietary cleaner. DON'T leave any polish on the silver after cleaning – it will encourage the surface to tarnish again.

★ Dip cleaners are useful for cutlery and for etched and embossed silver, but over-use will cause it to become dull.

★ Reach into deep crevices with cotton wool wrapped round a cuticle stick.

★ A drop of white spirit on a cotton wool bud will give your silver a quick shine when you're in a hurry.

Homemade cleaner

★ Dissolve a handful of soda crystals in a jug of hot water and add a handful of milk bottle tops or aluminium foil. Put your silver in the jug and leave for a few minutes – the tarnish will transfer itself from the silver to the foil. Rinse and dry thoroughly.

CLEANING SILVER/METALS

BRASS

★ Clean very dirty brass with a lemon dipped in vinegar and salt. Rinse thoroughly and clean with brass polish.

★ Ingrained dirt on **non-valuable** objects such as fire tongs should be rubbed with steel wool.

★ Clean the insides of brass preserving pans with vinegar and salt.

Never use metal polish on the inside of a pan used for cooking.

★ Lacquered brass should be washed occasionally in warm water and detergent. No polishing is needed.

CHROME

★ Wipe with a damp cloth and polish with a dry one.

★ Remove stubborn marks with a little vinegar or paraffin on a cloth.

★ Clean chrome teapots with a cloth dipped in vinegar and a little salt.

PEWTER

★ Pewter will collect a greyish bloom if kept in a damp atmosphere. Heavy oxide is often found on antique pieces and is better left uncleaned.

★ Polish pewter two or three times a year using fine wire wool and olive oil or a suitable proprietary polish.

STAINLESS STEEL

★ Wash in hot soapy water. Don't use metal scourers or scouring powders.

★ Shine pans by rubbing with a cut lemon or vinegar on a cloth.

COPPER

★ Wash copper utensils and ornaments with water and detergent. Rinse and dry well.

★ A homemade copper polish can be made of equal parts salt, vinegar and flour.

NOTE: Copper pans must be kept scrupulously clean because the patina can cause vomiting if eaten.

CLEANING FURNISHINGS

Removable furniture covers are usually washable and therefore more practical than fitted covers in households where there are children or pets. Follow the care label on the cover if there is one.

GENERAL ADVICE

* Remove any fringes or braiding before washing.
* Larger cotton and linen covers are best washed in a large launderette machine.
* Always iron covers on the

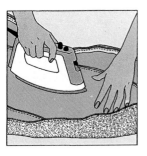

wrong side so that the fabric doesn't become shiny – except for glazed chintz, which shouldn't be ironed at all.
* Replace covers on chairs and sofas immediately after ironing, so that they take on the shape of the furniture while airing.
* All pile fabrics may be brushed lightly when dry.
* While you're washing loose covers, also vacuum and clean the furniture itself and wash or dry-clean cushions. Don't wash kapok-filled cushions – kapok becomes lumpy if it gets wet.

FABRIC GUIDE

Acrylics (eg Dralon): Warm wash, cold rinse, short spin. Iron if necessary with cool iron on wrong side.
Brocade: All brocades should be dry-cleaned.
Cotton: Machine-washable.
Glazed chintz: Dry-clean or machine-wash. Do not rub, twist or bleach. Do not iron or you'll destroy the glaze.
Linen: Hot wash, thorough rinse, spin dry. Can be starched. Iron with hot iron while still damp.
Rep: This can be cotton or cotton and synthetic fibres mixed. See care label. Wash as for weakest fibre.
Silk: Dry-clean taffetas and brocades. Other silks and

CLEANING FURNISHINGS

mixtures may be washed *very* carefully by hand. Dry indoors away from the sun. Do not soak in biological detergent. Do not use chlorine bleaches, although you can use hydrogen peroxide or sodium perborate if necessary. Iron with a cool iron while still damp.

Tweed: Dry-clean all-wool tweed. Wash synthetic-fibre tweeds as acrylic.

Velvet: Warm wash, short spin. (If in doubt, dry-clean.) To remove creases, hold over steam from kettle spout or iron on the wrong side and brush the pile gently.

Wool: Consult care label. If machine-washable, follow instructions carefully; otherwise dry-clean.

STRETCH COVERS

Warm wash, cool rinse, short spin. Drip-dry. Do not iron.

CURTAINS

★ Wash or clean curtains at least once a year.

★ Large, lined curtains become very heavy when wet, so it is usually easier to have them professionally cleaned. If you do wash them, pull both curtains and linings straight before hanging to dry. If curtains and linings are made of different fabrics, wash as for

the weakest constituent fabric.

★ Remove hardware (hooks, weights etc) before washing.

★ Hand-wash delicate fabrics.

★ Don't leave rayon or silk curtains to soak.

NET CURTAINS

★ Soak in the bath or sink.

★ Don't rub, twist or wring.

★ Whiten nylon with propietary net whitener.

★ Dip in starch to crisp.

★ Re-hang while still a little damp to avoid ironing.

REPAIRS CHECKLIST

Keep a note of any building work, repairs, maintenance etc carried out to your home, with details of the date, the cost and the company who undertook it, together with comments for future reference. If any problem arises with work that has been carried out, keep this card with you when contacting the company. Keep any guarantees safely and renew them if necessary.

Job .... Date ....

Undertaken by ....

Address ....

....

.... Tel No ....

Cost ....

Comments for reference ....

....

....

Job .... Date ....

Undertaken by ....

Address ....

....

.... Tel No ....

Cost ....

Comments for reference ....

....

REPAIRS CHECKLIST

Job .... Date ....

Undertaken by ....

Address ....

....

.... Tel No ....

Cost ....

Comments for reference ....

....

....

Job .... Date ....

Undertaken by ....

Address ....

....

.... Tel No ....

Cost ....

Comments for reference ....

....

....

It's worth keeping a note of any work that has been carried out well, as a tried-and-tested name is always useful if you, or a neighbour, ever need a similar job attended to in future.

SMOKE ALARMS

Smoke alarms (sometimes also called smoke detectors) are simple to fit and relatively inexpensive to buy. As long as you choose a sensible position for your alarms and remember to test them regularly, they will make an invaluable addition to the safety of your home.

SPECIAL FEATURES

Before you make your choice, decide how many features you want to make use of. Although the alarms most commonly available vary only slightly in performance, some offer extra safety features which may be worth considering to make your home even safer. These include:

★ A flashing indicator light to show the unit is working and/or a manual test button.

★ An 'escape light' which comes on when the alarm is triggered. This provides emergency light to help you find your way to safety if a fire disrupts the electricity supply.

★ An override button which disables the alarm for a short time and then returns it to normal (useful when fumes from cooking or DIY work trigger the alarm by accident).

★ Interconnection with other alarms, so that if one unit sounds the others are automatically triggered throughout the house – invaluable in a large home.

BS 5446 PART 1 1990

Note:

★ Look out for the Kitemark or confirmation that the alarm was made to British Standard BS5446 part I.

★ The Home Office and fire brigades both recommend a minimum of two smoke alarms in a small house; more in a bigger or more rambling one.

SMOKE ALARMS

POSITIONING

★ The centre of a hall ceiling is a good site; if fire breaks out at night in the living room or kitchen, smoke is detected

before it gets upstairs.

★ A second alarm fitted to the landing ceiling should detect smoke from fires starting in bedrooms.

★ It's important that the alarm is loud enough to be heard from all rooms and to wake sleepers. Check that the sound it emits is shrill enough, or buy several interconnecting alarms to site in key positions. Larger houses will need several units anyway, fitted in any room where there is a potential source of fire. Always fit too many rather than too few.

★ Don't site the alarm near to a wall or corner, and make sure that it is accessible for you to test regularly.

INSTALLATION

Alarms are easy to fit and come supplied with easy-to-follow instructions. Most have similar installation principles:

★ Open the smoke alarm unit itself as indicated.

★ Mark screw holes in position on the ceiling with a pencil.

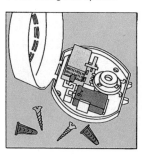

★ Use a screwdriver to attach screws to ceiling.

★ Fit detector over screws.

★ Reseal the unit.

MAINTENANCE

★ Test your alarms every few weeks.

★ Dust smoke alarm units regularly to keep them free from cobwebs etc.

★ Never paint over a smoke alarm.

★ Replace the batteries regularly as recommended by the manufacturers (usually once a year).

BREAK-INS & BURGLARIES

With any luck you'll never need to refer to this card, but if the worst happens, follow our checklist to keep the consequences as painless as possible.

Check your insurance cover BEFORE you need it. Don't go for the minimum cover just to keep premiums down. Discuss your requirements with the company and make sure that any valuables are listed separately from the main contents insurance. Choosing an index-linked 'new for old' policy means that cover is automatically upgraded each year to keep in line with current replacement prices. This means you won't have to reconsider your cover annually. It's also good to cover yourself against the theft of money from a snatched bag when you are away from home.

If you come home to discover that you have been burgled:

★ Call the police. Insurance companies always insist that thefts are reported.

★ If the police give you a job number, make sure you keep it safe as you may need to quote it later.

★ Don't touch anything until the police arrive, but make an initial check of what's missing.

★ Ask neighbours if they saw anyone behaving suspiciously or noticed a vehicle not usually seen locally. Tell the police anything you hear and ask them to check the details directly with your neighbours.

★ Make a detailed list of stolen goods to send to the insurance company.

★ Let the police have a duplicate list including codes marked on any items,

BREAK-INS & BURGLARIES

together with photographs of jewellery or antiques.

If you suspect that a burglar is still inside the house:

★ Don't go inside – some burglars react violently. Call 999 and report your suspicions to the police.

★ Make a note of anything suspicious near the scene including the number plates of any vehicles not normally seen in the area.

If you wake up and hear an intruder in the house:

★ Don't confront a burglar – he may be carrying a knife or other weapon.

★ Don't pretend to be asleep. Switch on the lights and make a lot of noise. If you're alone in the house, call out as if someone else is there. Dial 999 as soon as you safely can.

If your bag is snatched:

★ Let it go – you may be hurt in a tussle.

★ Report the loss to the closest police station and keep the job number given to you, in case you need to quote it later. Insurance companies always insist that a theft is reported.

★ Call your bank to stop any cheques left in the bag. Contact credit card agencies (remember to keep all the relevant telephone numbers in a safe place at home).

★ Remember that if your bag held keys and references to your address, the thief will have access to your home, so you may want to change door locks.

★ When claiming from the insurance company, remember that you can claim for your possessions – the handbag, and purse or wallet – as well as the money stolen, if you are covered for personal effects.

Telephone hotlines

★ If a credit card is lost or stolen, use these telephone numbers to report it immediately:

Barclaycard **0604 230230**
Access **0702 352255**
Diners Club **0252 513500**
American Express
0273 696933

If your car is broken into:

★ Report the incident to the nearest police station, even if nothing has been stolen.

★ Give details of codes if you have etched these on windows, wing mirrors or lights. Give serial numbers or codes etched on radio or cassette machines. Keep the job number safe.

★ Refer to your insurance details for any claims.

ALWAYS LOCK YOUR CAR – 25 per cent of stolen cars are left unlocked.

MOVING DAY CHECKLIST

The day before

❏ Prepare a survival kit to carry in the car with you: meals and drinks for the day, kettle, spoons, towels, soap, loo paper, candles, matches, can opener and first-aid kit.

❏ Pack overnight bags with necessities for your first night – even if you'll be staying in your new home rather than a hotel.

❏ Put house plants in a cardboard box to take with you in the car.

❏ Defrost and dry out fridge/freezer, and pack any remaining perishables in an insulated bag.

❏ Set your freezer on maximum if you're moving it with its contents intact.

❏ Make sure that you have money for petrol, meals, phone calls and tips for the removers.

❏ Take pets to neighbours or kennels to keep them safely out of the way during the move. Collect them

when you are ready for them in your new home.

❏ Leave babies and very young children with family or friends for the day of the move.

❏ Do last-minute washing and/or tumble drying before the washing machine is unplumbed.

❏ Collect any dry-cleaning.

❏ Dismantle self-assembly furniture and take down curtains and blinds.

On the day

❏ Show the removers around the house, including garage and shed. Explain your labelling system and

HOUSEHUNTERS' GUIDELINES

❑ Is there an outside television aerial?

❑ Are fences and guttering in good repair?

❑ Check for any damp patches, raised tiles, crumbling chimney-stacks, cracks in brickwork.

Flats

❑ Ask about maintenance charges. Who is responsible for upkeep of garden, roof, drains?

❑ If there's a shared entrance hallway, who cleans it, and how is it maintained?

❑ How are bills for the shared areas split? Are hall and stair lights on a timer?

❑ How much noise from the shared stairway penetrates the flat?

Kitchen

❑ Is there sufficient storage or room for more units?

❑ Is there plumbing – and enough space – for washing machine/dishwasher?

❑ Ask to see guarantees for fitted equipment such as the cooker.

❑ Can you smell anything from neighbours' kitchens?

❑ Do the windows or a fan bring in enough fresh air, or could condensation be a problem?

Bathroom

❑ Are there smells from the plug holes?

❑ How well does the loo flush? Try it.

❑ Are there leaking taps?

❑ Cracks in the ceramics?

❑ Is there adequate lighting?

Bedrooms

❑ Will your bed and wardrobe fit through the door or window?

❑ Is the existing furniture hiding damp patches?

❑ How thick are the walls? Will you be disturbed by neighbours' television, hi-fi or plumbing?

❑ Is there adequate storage space?

General

❑ Is the loft insulated?

❑ Cellar should be humid – but not damp.

❑ How efficient is central heating? Is there a timer?

❑ Are the rooms the right size for your furniture?

❑ Do the rooms have good natural light?

❑ Are windows double-glazed? Do they let in draughts and/or noise?

EMERGENCY CONTACT CARD

Keep this as a record of all emergency contacts, separate from your normal address book.

PLUMBING

Plumber: ....

....

....

Institute of Plumbing, 64 Station Lane, Hornchurch, Essex RM12 6NB (04024 72791). Has list of qualified members and will take up complaints made against a member.

GAS

Qualified fitter ....

....

....

British Gas Corporation .....

....

Local showrooms sell gas appliances, provide information, planning advice, lists of registered installers.

Institution of Gas Engineers, 17 Grosvenor Crescent, London SW1X 7ES (071-245 9811). Can supply list of qualified members who conform to standard code of practice.

ELECTRICITY

Electrician: ....

....

....

Local Electricity Showroom...............................

Office of Electricity Regulation (OFFER), Hagley House, Hagley Road, Birmingham B16 8QG (021-456 2100). Will refer you to your nearest regional office to pursue complaints.

Electrical Contractors' Association, 34 Palace Court, London W2 4HY (071-229 1266; **Edinburgh** 031-455 5577). Guarantees work of members and completion of a job at quoted price if firm goes out of business.

FIRE

Local Fire Brigade.................

....

Will give advice on fire prevention. **If fire has broken out though, always dial 999.**

Fire Protection Association, 140 Aldersgate Street, London EC1A 4HX (071-606 3757). Advice on fire prevention.

BUILDING AND DECORATION

Builder/Handyman: ....

....

....

....

Federation of Master Builders, 14 Great James Street, London WCIN 3DP (071-242 7583). For lists of local, qualified, builders. Also nine regional offices.

The Building Centre, Showroom and Bookshop, 26 Store Street, London WI. Visit for displays of modern building products.

Building Employees Confederation, 82 New Cavendish St, London WIM 8AD (071-580 5588). Will recommend members.

Women and Manual Trades, 52 Featherstone St, ECIY 8RT (071-251 9192). Register of skilled tradeswomen, including plumbers, carpenters, builders, decorators.

GENERAL

Doctor ....

....

Dentist ....

....

School ....

....

Vet ....

....

EMERGENCY SUPPLIES

You can help avoid domestic disasters by keeping a supply of tools and equipment to help you cope in an emergency:

- ☐ Bucket
- ☐ Extension reel
- ☐ First-aid kit
- ☐ Torch and batteries
- ☐ Rope
- ☐ Plumber's waterproof tape
- ☐ Spare ball float
- ☐ Sink and loo plunger
- ☐ Residual current device
- ☐ Rubber gloves
- ☐ Tap washers
- ☐ Fire extinguisher and blanket
- ☐ Polythene dust sheet
- ☐ Pipe cutter
- ☐ Blow torch
- ☐ Pipe bender
- ☐ Fuses and fuse wire
- ☐ Insulation tape
- ☐ Connector blocks
- ☐ Circuit tester
- ☐ Mains-tester screwdriver

IN CASE OF FIRE

PREVENTION IS BETTER THAN CURE

★ Always protect fires with wire guards.

★ Don't smoke in bed.

★ Don't leave matches or lighters where children can get them.

★ Make sure that you have smoke alarms in all rooms, working fire extinguishers and an escape route other than the main stairs. Your local fire prevention officer may help with advice.

Don't wait till disaster strikes. Be prepared for an emergency and make sure the whole household is familiar with the drill.

BURNING FOAM FURNITURE

This can emit poisonous fumes which kill within minutes.
If you catch the fire *very* early, douse with water.
Otherwise GET OUT of the building quickly.

CLOTHES ON FIRE

Smother the flames by rolling on the floor or, better still, rolling up tightly in a rug, blanket or heavy fabric.
When flames are out, remove the rug.
DO NOT try to remove burned-on clothes – leave that to the hospital.

CHIP PAN FIRE

Certain oils will ignite spontaneously at high temperatures. The safest frying oils are peanut, corn, sesame and sunflower. If the oil begins to smoke, turn down the heat at once. If the oil catches fire the procedure to follow is to **COOL the pan** and **SMOTHER the flames**:

1. Turn off the heat under the pan.
2. **DO NOT** move the pan.
3. **DO NOT** pour water over the flames.

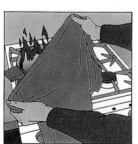

4. Smother the flames with a fire blanket or cover with a large lid, plate, tin tray, bread board or a damp (not wet) towel.

IN CASE OF FLOOD

PREVENTION IS BETTER THAN CURE

★ Make sure pipes are well lagged so they won't freeze and burst in winter.

★ Plumb in washing machines and dishwashers so they don't have to empty into a basin.

There's always a risk of leaving a plug in or the outlet becoming blocked.

★ Check condition of ballcock in cistern regularly and change it if necessary.

★ Locate your stop-cock.

BURST PIPE

Stop the flow of water at the stop-cock. (You should find this under the sink or near the bottom of the cold water tank or even outside the house.) Then turn on taps to drain the pipe. Call plumber.

OVERFLOW

If there is an overflow from the basin, lavatory or bath, turn off taps; stop washing machine; pull out plugs etc.

IN ALL CASES

1 Mop up excess water as quickly as possible with towels, bath mats, curtains, anything absorbent.
When saturated, put them in the bath to be dealt with later.

2 If water has saturated floor, ceiling or walls, turn off the electricity at the mains until the wiring has dried out.

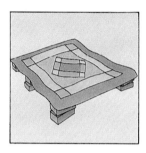

3 Lift carpet or other flooring if the water has got into or under it. Antique carpets should be dried and cleaned professionally as soon as possible. Other carpets should be laid on bricks or across chairs to air properly.

4 Open all windows and (when the wiring has dried out) run a fan heater in the room until everything is thoroughly dry.

5 Books, records etc should be given as much air as possible and gentle fan heat – but direct heat will warp them. Gently fan book pages while drying, to separate them.

6 Check with your insurance company whether you are liable for compensation.

NOTE: If the flood is from a river, the water will be muddy and leave a dank smell. You will have to redecorate and clean upholstery and cushions very thoroughly.

FLOODING FROM OUTSIDE

1 Turn off electricity, gas and water.

2 Block all exterior doors with polythene bags filled with rolled up blankets. Block all ground-floor window sills similarly.

3 Carry valuables, rugs and food upstairs to a dry place.

A GAS EMERGENCY

PREVENTION IS BETTER THAN CURE

★ Check that you know how and where to turn off the gas at the mains.

★ Keep flues and chimneys clear of soot and debris that could catch fire.

★ Keep gas fire mantles free of fluff.

★ Do not block the inlet grilles of radiant convector heaters with drying clothes as they will prevent air flowing and overheating of elements could result.

★ Get the jets cleaned occasionally by a qualified fitter.

★ Put wire fireguards round radiant elements to keep children away.

★ Make sure all appliances and connections are correctly installed.

★ Check from time to time for any loose taps and worn connecting tubing.

★ Keep a torch (with working batteries!) near the mains tap in case of emergency.

IF YOU SMELL GAS

1 Open all doors and windows.

2 Extinguish any naked flames – cigarettes, candles, gas pilot lights etc.

3 **DO NOT** light a match to see what's going on.

4 Test for leaks by smearing a strong solution of concentrated washing-up liquid over the hose or pipe. It will bubble where the gas is leaking.

5 Check that all gas taps and pilot lights on gas cooker, boiler etc are turned off.

6 If all seems to be in order and there's still a smell of gas, turn off the supply at the mains and call the Gas Service (under GAS in the telephone book). **NOTE**: It is both dangerous and illegal to try to mend a gas leak yourself.

7 If there is a very strong smell of gas, don't switch electric switches on or off: the minutest spark could cause an explosion. The same applies to using the telephone. Phone for help from an outside phone.
8 In the event of fire, follow the HOMEFAX procedure for FIRE.

AN ELECTRICAL EMERGENCY

PREVENTION IS BETTER THAN CURE

★ Always use equipment with the correct fuse.

★ Always make sure the wiring is correct and in good condition. Frayed wiring should be changed at once.

★ Always change damaged plugs and sockets immediately.

★ Never leave wires trailing.

★ Never overload a socket.

★ Keep a torch and spare fuses by the electricity meter/mains switch.

★ If there are children in your home, cover unused sockets with tape or socket covers.

★ NEVER use electrical equipment in the bathroom or touch with wet hands.

ELECTRICAL FIRES

1 Switch off electricity at the mains.

2 Extinguish the fire with an all-purpose extinguisher or one designed specifically for electrical fires.

3 If you have no suitable extinguisher, smother the flames with a heavy rug or blanket.

NOTE: DO NOT apply water unless you know that the mains current is switched off, and NEVER use water on a TV or computer – residual current may give you a shock even if the machine is turned off.

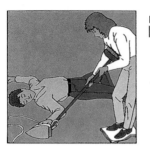

ELECTRIC SHOCK
1 DO NOT go near the casualty until you are sure there's no danger to yourself. EITHER switch off power at mains OR put on rubber soled shoes, stand on a wad of folded newspaper, and knock casualty clear of the electric contact with a broom handle or other insulated object.

2 Dial 999 and ask for 'Ambulance'.

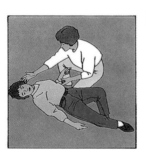

3 If the casualty is unconscious, check breathing. Give mouth-to-mouth and chest compression if necessary. Learn the first-aid procedure in advance.
If unconscious, turn person over on back and raise legs to get the blood flowing back to the heart.

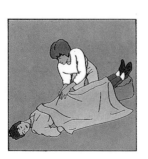

4 Hold any burns under running water or immerse in bucket of clean cold water.

5 Consult first-aid manual for treatment for shock. Give no food or drink. Reassure casualty. Wrap in blanket. Wait for ambulance.

CHANGING A TAP WASHER

There are two basic types of tap that need new washers when they start to drip: traditional cross-top (capstan-head) taps or modern, chunky, shroud-headed taps. If a tap with ceramic discs leaks, it's usually because a piece of grit has got between the discs and the problem should be dealt with by a professional.

CHOOSING A WASHER

Basin and sink taps have 12mm (½in) washers; bath taps have 19mm (¾in) washers. There are hard rubber or leather washers for hot taps, soft ones for cold taps or plastic for either. Rubber washers can be cut to fit with a craft knife.

CROSS-TOP TAP

1 Turn off the water supply at the stopcock and turn on the tap to let the water drain out.
2 Unscrew the top part of the tap (the shroud). If it sticks, pour over boiling water. If it still sticks, bang it with a spanner wrapped in a cloth.

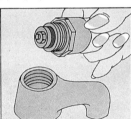

3 Unscrew the main nut holding the main body of the tap and lift it clear.

4 Unscrew the nut holding the washer.

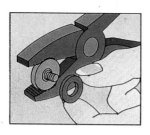

5 Remove the washer and replace it with the new one.

6 Screw all the parts of the tap together as before.
7 Turn on the water at the stopcock.

SHROUD-HEADED TAP
Moulded acrylic tap tops may be fixed with a main screw hidden under the H or C disc, which will have to be prised off. Or they may simply pull off with a sharp tug. From then on, work as for cross-top taps.

TOOLS AND MATERIALS
You will need an adjustable spanner, washers (or 'jumpers' for supataps), available from plumbers' suppliers.

CHANGING A TAP WASHER

SUPATAPS

These are not often used now. If your house has them, you do not have to turn the water off to change the washer, or 'jumper'.

3 Gently press the knob on the spout onto a worktop to release the nozzle and jumper.

1 Loosen the top nut with a spanner.

2 Turn the tap on and on and on until the handle comes off. At this stage the valve will automatically stop the flow of water to the tap.

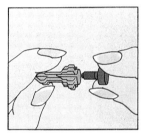

4 Turn the nozzle upside down and the jumper will fall out. Remove it with a screwdriver, clean the nozzle with a nailbrush and fit a new jumper.
5 Screw all the parts together as before.

GENERAL TAP MAINTENANCE

All taps should be washed regularly to avoid corrosion. Polish with a soft cloth (do not use abrasives.)

Always match replacement washers to the size of the existing ones and remove all pieces of the old one.

Encourage children to turn off taps firmly: a dripping tap in a hard-water area will stain the sink. To remove persistent stains, rub with half a fresh lemon.

If you are fitting new taps, bear in mind the people who will be using them: children and the elderly can have difficulty in handling some designs.

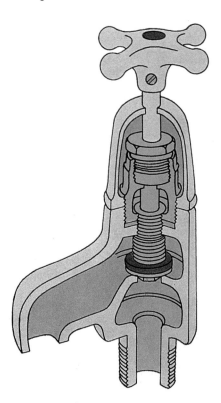

WASTE-PIPES AND DRAINAGE

MAINTAINING INDOOR WASTE-PIPES

Most kitchen sink blockages are caused by grease, hair and kitchen debris. These build up gradually in traps and waste-pipes, causing obstructions, sluggish water drainage and unpleasant smells.

★ To maintain indoor waste-pipes, avoid pouring fat or cooking oil down the kitchen sink drain and use a sink tidy for scraps. Install drain-hole strainers on bathroom plug-holes to stop hair and soap scum clogging waste pipes.

CLEARING WASTE-PIPES AND SHIFTING MINOR BLOCKAGES

★ Although caustic soda (in jelly or crystal-form) is often recommended for dissolving debris, this is a strong chemical cleaning agent which can damage textiles, paintwork and tiles and should not come into contact with the skin or eyes. You should always use caustic soda with care – wear rubber gloves and follow the manufacturer's instructions to the letter.

★ A gentler (and greener) alternative for minor blockages and regular cleaning is to use washing soda crystals. Empty about a quarter of a standard

1kg packet of washing crystals around the plug-hole and then pour on a kettle-full of very hot water. (Do not let the crystals come into contact with aluminium.)

USING A PLUNGER

If the water fails to drain from one sink, basin or bath in the house, while all the others are working normally, the obstruction must be in its own branch pipe. Try forcing the blockage out of the pipe by using a sink plunger – they're available from hardware and DIY stores:

1 To prevent air escaping through the overflow, stop it up with a wet cloth.

2 Make sure that there's enough water in the sink to cover the plunger's rubber cup. (If the sink's badly blocked, it will be full of water anyway!)

WASTE PIPES & DRAINAGE

3 Hold the wet cloth in the overflow with one hand while you pump the handle of the plunger up and down.

4 If the water in the sink doesn't drain away immediately, the blockage may simply have been pushed a little further along the pipe, so try using the plunger again. If you don't have a plunger, try improvising by using a plastic bag, tied around the head of a mop or round a sponge tied to a stick.

CLEARING THE WASTE-PIPE TRAP

If the sink is still blocked, you may need to clear the trap. This is situated under the sink and it's common for debris to collect at the lowest point of the pipe's bend.

1 Place a bucket under the sink (or a tray if you're unblocking a bath pipe) to catch any water and debris that may be released.

2 Put the plug in the plug-hole.

3 Use a spanner or wrench to release the 'cleaning eye' or access cap on the U of the trap.

4 If your trap is bottle rather than U-shaped, unscrew the access cap by hand.

(If there is no way that you can gain access to this part of the trap, unscrew the connecting nuts, remove the whole trap and then rinse it out.)

5 The contents of the trap (including the debris that is causing the blockage) should now drain into your bucket or tray.

MAJOR BLOCKAGES

Any major blockages involving exterior drains are often best left to the professionals.

★ If your house is individually drained, the whole system is your responsibility until it joins the main sewer.

★ If your exterior drain is linked to other homes, contact your environmental health officer to find out whether you are responsible for maintaining the drains.

Local councils should cleanse drains constructed before 1937, but this service isn't always free.

Communal drainage systems constructed after 1937 are the responsibility of all the householders concerned (so you and your neighbours will have to share the cost of repairs up to the sewer, no matter where the fault occurs).

LAGGING PIPES

Check for: unlagged pipes, especially in exposed areas. (For unlagged water cisterns and radiators that don't heat up properly, see over.)

LAGGING PIPES

Tools and materials
Scissors, sharp knife, felt strip or plastic foam, string, waterproof adhesive tape. Flexible foam plastic comes in sizes to fit any pipe between 6mm (¼in) and 75mm (3in) diameter. Always use the correct size for the pipe.

Felt lagging
1 Wind round three times at tank end and bind with string.
2 Wrap strip diagonally, overlapping edges.

3 Bind each new strip of felt with string where it overlaps the previous one (above right).
4 Wrap lagging generously round neck of valves, stopcocks etc.

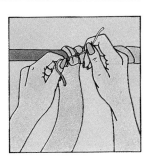

5 Lag overflow pipes, concentrating on area next to outside wall.

Foam lagging
1 Wrap as for felt, making sure edges are close together.
2 Fix with adhesive tape round tank end (below).
3 At bends, push and tape edges together.
4 To seal joints, overlap pieces of foam and tape together.

TANKS AND RADIATORS

LAGGING CISTERNS
Cold-water tanks
● Buy glass-fibre blanket material bonded with paper on one side for easier handling.

1 Cut to fit (if tank is very large, you may have to use two overlapping pieces).

2 Secure with string and/or adhesive tape. Tape may help to hold blanket in place while you adjust it.

3 Start at base and overlap ends by 75mm (3in).

4 Cut slots where pipes enter tank and tuck the cut edges under the pipes.

5 Cut out a piece of material to overlap lid by about 150mm (6in). Do not tie.

Hot-water cylinders
The cheapest lagging is an old duvet, but a ready-made jacket (available from builders' merchants) is neater.

CLEARING RADIATOR AIR LOCKS

If a radiator is not heating up properly, air has probably become trapped somewhere. Bleed the system while the water is warm by opening the vent valve until water runs out freely.

● Most radiators have a square-ended hollow key (obtainable from hardware shops) to open the vent valve.

1 Insert key and turn anti-clockwise.

2 Hold a jar under the valve to collect water.

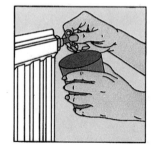

3 Tighten valve as soon as air stops escaping and water flows freely.

4 If necessary repeat process.

WASHING MACHINE CARE

A service engineer will charge just for the journey to your door, so it pays to look after your washing machine well and, if the fault is a simple one, to be able to correct it yourself.

PLUMBING IN
● If possible, get your washing machine plumbed into position permanently, so you won't have to manoeuvre it to the sink and attach hoses to the taps whenever you want to launder.

● Drainage hoses are supplied with machines to drain into the sink, but this can sometimes cause flooding. Plumbing it into a waste connection below the sink is far more sensible.

● If in doubt about your water pressure level, check with the local water authority before installation. Pressure can sometimes be adjusted by a special valve but this must be checked with the machine manufacturer.

SAFETY NOTES
● ALWAYS remove the electric plug from the socket before carrying out any maintenance or repairs.
● MAKE SURE the floor is waterproof (especially in an upstairs room) as flooding is always a possibility.
● DO NOT attempt any more complicated jobs than those suggested here.

LIKELY FAULTS
If your machine fails to function at all:
1 Check the fuse in the plug and replace it if necessary. Make sure the new fuse is the correct amperage. A blown fuse indicates a fault somewhere, so check the plug and wiring too, and if necessary call in the service engineer.
2 Check the flex and fit a new one if it is damaged.

If the machine is leaking:
Check the hose and replace any damaged part with copper tubing of exactly the same internal diameter as the hose (see instructions overleaf).

WASHING MACHINE CARE

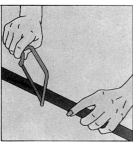

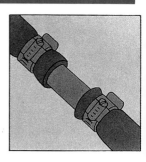

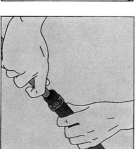

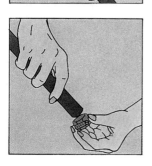

attached to the machine.

2 Slide a hoseclip onto the hose and tighten it to secure the tube.

3 Pass a hoseclip over the other section of hose, push in the other end of the copper tube and tighten it.

If the drier of a twin-tub spins erratically:

Look between the drum and the barrel to see if any small items such as socks are caught there. If so, fish them out carefully with a wire coat-hanger.

NOTE: If you suspect the problem is caused by any of the following, call in the service engineer:

● Faulty switches.
● Motor windings.
● Brushes.
● Brake cable.
● Brake linings.
● Drive belt.
● Heating element.

1 Saw off the damaged part with a hacksaw. Fit a length of copper tube into the end still

WIRING A THREE-PIN PLUG

Modern plugs have an integral cartridge fuse which should always be the weak link and therefore the 'safe' thing to blow if there's anything wrong with the house wiring or an individual electrical appliance. So NEVER use a fuse of a higher amperage than recommended for a particular plug or appliance.

TOOLS AND MATERIALS

Sharp craft knife or (preferably) wire strippers; wire cutters; small screwdriver; correct-amp cartridge fuse.

WIRING THE PLUG

1 Unscrew the plug cover and lever out the fuse.

2 Unscrew the little bar at the bottom of the plug. This is to clamp the flex in place.

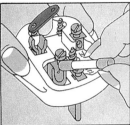

3 Cut away 50mm (2in) of the outer plastic of the flex so the coloured wires stick out; fix these under the clamp.

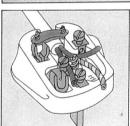

4 Cut each wire to reach about 12mm (½in) beyond the correct terminal (check the colours), then strip about 6mm (¼in) of coloured plastic away.

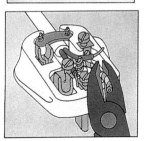

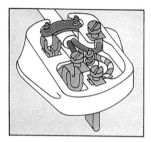

5 Twist the strands of each wire together and fit them into the loopholes (if the plug has them) or loop them clockwise round the terminals. Make sure you don't leave any stray wires.

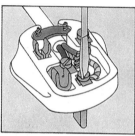

6 Tighten screws.
7 Fit correct fuse.
8 Make a final check that wires are connected to correct terminals and screw on cover.

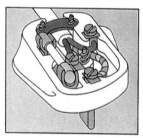

COLOUR CODES
For safety, learn the colours of the different wires by heart:
Green and Yellow = earth
Blue = neutral
Brown = live
On the plug, earth is marked E or ⏚, neutral is marked N and live is marked L/i. You MUST attach the right wires to the right terminals.

NOTE 1: Always use the fuse recommended by appliance manufacturers. As a general rule, use a 3amp fuse for most electric blankets, power tools, record players, clocks, standard lamps. Use a 13amp fuse for almost everything else.

NOTE 2: Continental and American equipment is designed for a lower voltage than our 220-240 range, so unless the appliance is officially imported over here you must use a transformer.

KNOW YOUR OWN FUSE BOX

Electricity comes into the house via a mains cable to the Electricity Board's sealed meter and then to a 'consumer unit' (consisting of your mains switch and fuse box). It is illegal and dangerous to tamper with the sealed meter.

A typical consumer unit contains six fuse carriers: a 30-amp or 45-amp fuse for the cooker, two 30-amp fuses for socket outlet ring circuits, a 15-amp fuse for a hot-water immersion heater and two 5-amp fuses for upstairs and downstairs lighting circuits.

In the ring circuit (ring-main) system, a cable runs from the fuse box around the house, linking sockets and ending back at the fuse box. There may be more than one ring circuit in your house, although each one must have its own 30-amp fuse. Ceiling and fixed wall lights are always on a separate 5-amp circuit.

Some older houses do not have consumer units. Instead they have a separate mains switch for cooker, lighting, water-heating and perhaps a mains switch and multi-way fuse board for power sockets. Remember that, if your wiring is more than 25 years old, it is recommended that you have it checked by a qualified electrical contractor.

FUSES

★ If there's a fault, the fuse being the weakest link will 'blow' first, breaking the electrical circuit and minimising the risk of fire.

★ Always use fuse wire of the correct amp rating.

★ Some fuse boxes have mains circuit-breakers instead of fuses which switch off the supply if there's a fault. Others use cartridge fuses rather than a rewirable fuse carrier.

★ Keep torch near fuse box with wire cutters, screwdriver and spare fuse wire: 5-amp for lighting, 30-amp for power circuits and 3- and 13-amp cartridge fuses for plugs.

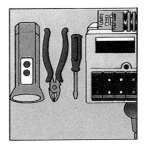

KNOW YOUR OWN FUSE BOX

CIRCUIT FAILURE

A failure in several lights or fittings at once means that one of the circuit fuses has blown in the mains fuse box. The cause may be a faulty socket, plug or appliance, an overloading of the circuit, or a fault in the actual wiring of the circuit.

★ To rewire a blown fuse: Remove the old wire and any blobs of metal, loop the new wire clockwise round the screw at one end, pass it through the holder and loop it clockwise round the screw at the other end.

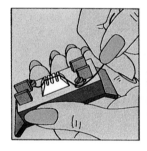

★ If a circuit-breaker fuse has 'tripped' (switched off), just switch it on again, once you have sorted out the problem.

★ In the case of a cartridge-type mains circuit fuse, simply replace with a new fuse.

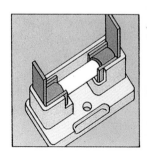

JANUARY GARDEN DIARY

VEGETABLES

★ Growing crops such as parsley, winter lettuce and spinach may need protecting from bad weather. Cover with cloches or, if the area is reasonably sheltered from high winds, rig up your own protectors from heavy-gauge polythene, making sure it is tightly secured.

★ Plant shallots.

★ Complete winter digging as soon as possible.

FRUIT

★ Prune hardy bush fruits and trees, but leave those producing stone fruits until later in the year.

★ Use light netting or strands of cotton to protect bushes and cane fruit from birds.

★ It's a good time to renovate neglected apple trees. If extensive lopping is necessary, don't do it all in one season or the tree may go into shock. This is a big subject and you should seek further advice. Try *The Fruit Expert* by Dr D G Hessayon (pbi, £3.95).

GREENHOUSE

★ Take the opportunity of giving your greenhouse a good spring clean before new sowings take place, to remove any pests and diseases. Nip off any dead or diseased leaves from plants that will over-winter here. Scrub down the staging and the greenhouse with a garden disinfectant,

JANUARY GARDEN DIARY

and spray any borders with it, too – *after* removing the residue of last year's crops.

★ Get seed-sowing under way: for example, sweet peas, antirrhinum, begonias, lettuce, cabbage and cauliflower.

★ Use clean seed trays or pots, with broken crocks in the base for drainage. Cover with seed compost to within a half-inch of the top. Soak through and drain. Sow seeds thinly on surface. Cover lightly with compost and firm gently. Cover until first seedlings appear.

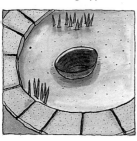

PONDS

★ Don't allow the pond to freeze over entirely if you keep fish. A pond heater will help, or a floating plastic ball or container which can be pulled out from the ice, leaving an air hole. Don't break the ice with a hammer – the fish could suffer.

TREES

★ Birds are a problem this month, so protect new-forming buds by covering the tree with netting.

★ Make sure your newly planted trees have not been loosened by bad weather. If so, just tread them in again firmly.

BULBS

★ If you have inherited a garden, it's worth sticking marker tags into the positions of early-flowering bulbs as they come up, to remind you of their positions later on.

FEBRUARY GARDEN DIARY

SHRUBS

★ Pruning starts this month, but only work on shrubs that bloom on the new season's growth, otherwise you'll jeopardise this year's blooms. Check a good reference book for your specific shrubs and climbers. Cut back winter jasmine after flowering. Prune summer-flowering clematis.

★ Shrubs may start enjoying some milder weather, but if a cold snap returns, be ready to re-cover against frost.

FLOWERS

★ Sow lobelia, impatiens, phlox and polyanthus in seed boxes, and raise under cover until the risk of frosts has passed.

★ Prick out the seedlings sown last month.

★ Plant roses towards the end of the month if the soil is not wet or frozen. Trim back roots by about 2in and prune back stems to leave three buds (with

the top bud facing outwards).

★ Fork over the established beds, removing all the weeds. Sprinkle on a general fertiliser such as Growmore.

★ New beds should be prepared by the end of this month to allow for the start of planting up. Only plant if the weather conditions are suitable. If not, leave in the shed and cover to protect them from the frost.

LAWNS

★ New turf should be laid by the end of this month.

★ If seeding a new lawn, prepare the site now for an April or May sowing.

★ Check that your mower is ready for use and complete any necessary repairs.

FRUIT

★ Feed trees, canes and bushes. Dig in garden compost or manure to help moisture

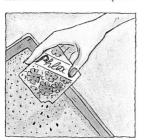

FEBRUARY GARDEN DIARY

retention later in the summer. Give a top dressing of general fertiliser.

PONDS

★ Spring may be in sight, but be vigilant about checking the pond for ice. For the sake of the fish, don't let it ice right over.

BULBS

★ Bulbs naturalised in grass will appreciate a light feed of bone-meal. Just sprinkle it on without getting heavy-handed.

HEDGES

★ Remove fallen leaves from the base of hedges, and take up invasive weeds.
★ Both bare-rooted deciduous plants and those that are container-grown can be planted now, as long as the earth is neither waterlogged nor frozen.
★ Make sure that newly planted hedging gets enough to

drink if the conditions are dry.
★ Cut back overgrown hedges.
★ Firm up any hedging plants that have been loosened by high winds.

ROCK GARDENS

★ When conditions are suitable, start tidying up the rockery. Herbaceous plants can

be cut back now. Leave woody plants such as heathers until it is warmer.
★ Remove any debris.
★ Firm in plants lifted by frost.
★ Take up any weeds before they have a chance to bed in.

GREENHOUSES

★ Sunnier days will increase the warmth inside the greenhouse. Remember to check that there is enough ventilation when it is needed. But reduce it again when the sun has gone.

MARCH GARDEN DIARY

SHRUBS

★ Annual pruning starts this month with a vengeance on plants that will flower on the new growth. Be careful not to prune those that bloom on last season's growth until *after* they have flowered, or you may accidentally snip off some of the portions that would have bloomed.

FLOWERS

★ Towards the end of the month, hardy and half-hardy annuals can be sown in soil treated with a dressing of bonemeal. Draw the soil over lightly to cover them.

★ Prick out and pot up the seedlings that were sown last month. Leave them in a covered cold frame unless the weather proves exceptionally warm, in which case you can raise the lid, but remember to cover the frame again at night or if frost is forecast.

ROSES

★ This is a good time for rose pruning, but take care if frosty conditions prevail.

★ You may need to protect roses from hungry rabbits.

LAWNS

★ Check whether there are any signs of the lawn having lifted during frosty conditions. If so, run a roller over it to flatten it back.

★ Unless conditions are too wet, you can start mowing the lawn, but only use the blades on their high setting.

MARCH GARDEN DIARY

★ Check the lawn regularly for signs of weeds and nip them out as soon as they appear, before they can take hold.

★ Apply lawn feed unless the weather is unsuitable.

FRUIT

★ Prune fruits such as plums, damsons and cherries. Apply wound paint to the cuts.

★ Pruning is a large subject, and a good practical manual like *The Fruit Expert* by Dr D G Hessayon (pbi) should be consulted before starting.

★ Alpine strawberry seeds may be sown now, but protect them either under a cloche or in the greenhouse.

PONDS

★ Don't be fooled by the warmer weather – there could still be a nasty frost for some time to come. So check that the pond has not frozen up.

★ Pond planting can take place

now – either in special aquatic baskets, or direct into soil at the bottom. Baskets are easier because they can be lifted out to replant and prune. Baskets also restrict plant growth, slowing down the rate at which they can overgrow a pond.

ROCK GARDENS

★ A good time to plant new alpines in the rock garden – it should be neither too hot nor too cold for them.

★ Check that the plants are still protected from slugs.

VEGETABLES

★ Sow seeds of asparagus, carrot, broad bean, sprouts, peas, radish, celery, turnip and beetroot.

GREENHOUSE

More vegetables can be sown under glass, such as cabbages and leeks. Check the seed packet for the precise timing.

APRIL GARDEN DIARY

SHRUBS

★ Neglected shrubs such as deutzia, forsythia, syringa and philadelphus can be given a drastic prune to try getting them back into shape. Cut the whole shrub back to ground level, unless there are year-old shoots growing from the base. Leave these, and cut down the rest. Don't despair if the shrub doesn't recover – it's better to lose it and start again, than to keep an inferior specimen.

★ Check that the ties on wall-growing plants are secure before summer growth.

★ Prune early-flowering shrubs once blooming has finished.

★ Don't remove shrubs that look frost dead – new growth may appear this month once the plant has recovered.

CLIMBERS

★ Clematis can be planted, but you should protect their roots

from the sun with other shrubs or a paving slab. The rest of the plant will enjoy full sunshine.

FLOWERS

★ Sow hardy annuals outside from the middle of the month if the soil is dry enough.

★ Seedlings potted last month should be coming along well. Leave them in the cold frame until the danger of frost is past.

★ Divide overgrown perennials by splitting into two or more pieces and replanting where required. Unwanted pieces can be given away to other gardeners.

★ Once the soil has warmed up, apply a mulch around perennials to suppress weeds and hold in moisture.

★ Stake plants as soon as they need it for support.

ROSES

★ Any established roses will benefit from a dressing of rose fertiliser. And a good organic mulch applied round the main stem will both feed the plant and conserve moisture.

LAWNS

★ Grass will begin to grow more quickly now, and you will need to increase the frequency of mowing. The blades can be lowered to about 12mm (½in).

APRIL GARDEN DIARY

★ Remove weeds before they can take hold.

★ New lawns may be sown in the last week if weather conditions are suitable. It's a good time to repair damaged or worn areas.

FRUIT

★ Fruits grown in a container

will appreciate a regular dose of a liquid potassium-based fertiliser such as those given to tomatoes.

★ Keep strawberries protected from frost for the rest of the month.

VEGETABLES

★ Put your first sowings of lettuce in this month, and keep sowing at monthly intervals to ensure a crop throughout the summer and autumn.

★ Sow melons now – I seed to a 7.5cm (3in) pot of moist potting compost. Cover tightly with polythene or cling film and pop into the airing cupboard. Check each day for germination and, at the first signs, remove polythene and place pots on a windowsill until you plant them out in June.

★ Sow tomato seeds thinly in shallow seed trays, and prick out singly into 3in pots when seedlings have two leaves. Keep indoors or in the greenhouse for the time being.

PONDS

★ Clean out if dirty. Remove plants, house fish in temporary quarters and empty pool to clean it. Divide and prune plants before returning them to the pool.

★ To return fish to the pool, or to add new ones, place them with some of their water in plastic bags and seal. Place bags in pond. Leave a couple of hours for the temperatures to equalise before releasing fish.

MAY GARDEN DIARY

SHRUBS

★ Clear any weeds from around shrubs, then give them an application of a good general fertiliser.

★ Water shrubs well, especially if they are newly planted. Then cover the soil over with plenty of well-rotted organic compost as a mulch to help conserve the moisture.

★ If the soil is wet enough, plant ball or container-grown evergreens such as holly (if the soil is still cold, you'll find that it's best to wait until the autumn).

★ Watch out for aphids, and spray if necessary.

ROSES

★ If you haven't already done so, replace any damaged roses with container-grown plants while you still can. Don't disturb roots when planting as the rose will be well on in its growing cycle.

★ It's a prime time for aphids on roses, so make sure you spray now in time to prevent a plague later.

CLIMBERS

★ Growth starts to become vigorous about now. Tie in as necessary and prune any wayward shoots that spoil the overall profile of the plant.

FLOWERS

★ Take your seedlings to their next stage. Depending on when you started them, they'll need pricking out or potting on.

★ Before planting out those grown in a greenhouse, harden off by acclimatising them to cooler conditions gradually.

LAWNS

★ Much early spring work on the lawn will be completed, but it's still necessary to give it some attention.

★ Adjust height of cutter to about ½in for summer.

★ If drought conditions develop, raise the cutter height a little. If the grass becomes too dry, stop cutting altogether.

★ Give another application of weed and moss killers if necessary.

★ Lawns will need a *weekly* water for as long as possible. (Daily light applications of

MAY GARDEN DIARY

water can actually be *un*helpful, since the grass tends to grow only shallow roots instead of the life-saving deeper roots.)

ROCK GARDENS

★ Rockery alpines are now at their peak.
★ Early bulbs will be dying down – allow foliage to die naturally.
★ Keep weeds down.
★ Don't overwater. Keep alpines on the dry side to encourage their roots to grow down, enabling them to search deep for moisture. This will stand them in good stead

during drought conditions.
★ To propagate, collect seeds from early-flowering varieties, and store in paper bags in a cool, dry place until sowing time. (Check individual sowing times for each plant variety.)

VEGETABLES

★ Sow runner beans towards the end of the month. If space is limited, grow them up a wigwam of four or more 8ft bamboo canes tied together at the top. Two seeds can be grown at the foot of each cane.
★ Sow sweetcorn in groups 15in apart to form a block that aids pollination. Plant three seeds in each group, and later remove the two weakest plants, leaving the strong one to develop on. Water well when in flower and when the cobs are forming.

PONDS

★ Plant container-grown pond plants.
★ Weed where necessary, but remember plants are now too far advanced to lift and divide.
★ Fish can be introduced as long as new plants are established.
★ Algae will form after the pond is cleaned and refilled. The leaves of spreading plants will help inhibit algae growth.

JUNE GARDEN DIARY

SHRUBS

* If we have a dry month, continue giving shrubs a good long soak for as long as possible – water shortages permitting.
* Any early-flowering shrubs flowering on last year's wood will need pruning once they have bloomed.

FLOWERS

* Now's the time you may notice gaps in your perennial border. One solution is to interplant with annuals while you wait for the perennials to fill out and take over the gaps.
* Deadhead regularly.
* Long shoots and tall plants may need staking. Do this before rough weather can batter them down.
* Keep weeds under control.
* When aubrietia has finished flowering, give it a 'haircut' with shears. Remove old growth for even better flowers next year.

* When foliage has died right down, spring-flowering bulbs can be lifted and stored in a dry place ready for replanting in the autumn.

HEDGES & TREES

* Plant container-grown hedge plants and trees this month, bearing in mind that if it is particularly dry they must be kept well watered.
* Prune any flowering hedges as soon as they have finished flowering.
* Check young trees to make sure their stake ties haven't become too tight with growth. If they have, slacken them off.

LAWNS

* The grass will need a regular mow and will benefit from scarifying – which removes dead 'thatch' from the lawn.
* If the lawn has become compacted by heavy wear, spike the surface and apply a

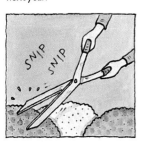

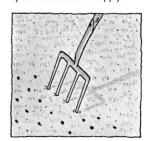

JUNE GARDEN DIARY

top dressing followed by plenty of watering.

FRUIT
★ Soft fruit will soon be ready, but make sure it is protected from the birds. Use fine-mesh plastic or Terylene netting, or buy a ready-made fruit cage.
★ Give special attention to strawberries. Protect the fruit from slugs and spread straw beneath the ripening fruit to keep it clean.

VEGETABLES
★ Sow marrows this month – three seeds every metre or so. When they have germinated, thin out by discarding the two weakest. Remember that you can also pick them when they reach an appropriate size to cook as courgettes.
★ Plant outdoor tomatoes 1 metre apart and stake. Water plentifully and often. Allow four flower 'trusses', or tufts,

to form, then pinch out the top growth to prevent any more forming. Pinch out side growths while young.

GREENHOUSE
★ Organise shading for hot weather – either using blinds or painting on a coat of white Coolglass (from garden centres).
★ Be prepared to turn on the heat again if necessary to protect your plants from unexpected frosts.
★ Use the greenhouse to propagate new plants. Dip cuttings in hormone rooting powder, then pot up in cutting composts.

PONDS
★ Algae and weeds grow prolifically from now on and will need controlling.
★ Complete planting of aquatic plants by the end of the month if possible.
★ Remove old spent leaves before they rot in the water.
★ Keep the pond topped up in hot weather if the water level shows signs of dropping.
★ Keep an eye on fish if the weather is hot and humid. If they come up for air, you can help them by aerating the water. Install a fountain or, as an interim measure, spray water on the surface of the pond.

JULY GARDEN DIARY

SHRUBS

★ Shrubs that flowered and were then pruned in the spring should now be showing their new growth.

★ Those that were pruned hard in the spring will be coming into flower.

★ Give both types a foliage feed of tomato fertiliser, or dress with sulphate of potash, watered in well.

★ Remove buddleia flowers as they die off, and you should get a second crop.

★ Give shrubs as much water as you can if we get a long hot dry spell.

★ Pests and diseases often manifest themselves on shrubs at this time. Keep checking, and deal with them if they show signs of attack.

ROSES

★ Deadhead regularly.

★ Give roses the season's final dressing of rose fertiliser to encourage more blooms.

★ General upkeep should be continued, such as weeding, tying back new growth, removing suckers and watching out for aphids, mildew and all the other problems that can beset roses.

FLOWERS

★ Remove dead flower heads daily if possible, to keep flowers blooming.

★ Keep up general maintenance such as weeding and tidying, so that the garden looks its best.

★ Take care where you put your feet when working in flower borders. It would be a pity to damage plants now, when such care has been put into nurturing their growth.

★ Take cuttings from pinks and carnations once the main flush of blooms has finished.

★ Delphiniums should be cut back to about 6in after

JULY GARDEN DIARY

flowering. Keep them damp, and they should flower once again in the autumn.

HEDGES

★ New hedge plants started in containers can be planted this month, but don't let them dry out in hot weather.

★ Box, hornbeam, gorse, holly and laurel can be pruned back.

★ Encourage new hedge plants to thicken up by trimming the plants back.

★ New conifers in particular will suffer in hot weather. Spray regularly with water.

FRUIT

★ Soft fruit is at its very best now. Harvest gooseberries, redcurrants, blackcurrants and raspberries. Cherries can be picked now, too.

★ Apples and pears will benefit if you thin out some of the little fruits that have set. This will help the trees

produce good-sized fruit later on. Some fruitlets will be shed naturally early in the month, so wait until this has happened before taking more off.

VEGETABLES

★ This month you will be seeing the benefit of all your earlier hard work. For the most succulent vegetables, crop as soon as ready.

★ Late sowings of beetroot, carrot, spinach and lettuce should be completed this month if you want to harvest a crop this year.

PONDS

★ Keep up general maintenance. Continue to take out excessive growth to stop the pond getting choked up. Top up if water level falls.

★ Keep an eye on your fish to make sure they are not suffering during hot weather. Keep the water aerated.

AUGUST GARDEN DIARY

SHRUBS

★ Continue to keep shrubs well watered, and check for signs of pests or disease.

★ On climbing shrubs, make sure that growth is not restricted by the ties securing the stems. Loosen them if necessary.

FLOWERS

★ Continue to deadhead on a regular basis and keep tidy.

★ Border carnations can be propagated by layering.

★ If your irises are becoming overcrowded, divide them now. Separate the new rhizomes from the old parent plant in the centre by pulling them away. Throw away the old plant. Trim each rhizome (both the foliage and the bottom of the stem). Plant each rhizome in its new position, leaving half showing above the soil. Keep them damp until established.

★ Everlasting flowers are likely to be ready for drying. Pick just before the flowers come into full bloom and choose a warm, dry day. Don't try to pick the flowers if the weather is wet, or when dew has formed.

★ You will probably need to put in your order for new roses now. Try to buy locally so that the plants are used to the climatic and soil conditions of your garden.

★ Apply a foliar feed to dahlias to help keep them growing prolifically. Spray them against aphids if necessary.

HEDGES

★ Choose and order bare-rooted plants now, for planting during the winter. Order a few more than you need in case you suffer losses and are unable to match up replacements.

★ Keep the bottoms of hedges weed-free.

AUGUST GARDEN DIARY

★ If you wish to resite a hedge, you can do it from mid-August onwards as long as the plants are healthy.

GREENHOUSE

★ Work should be done on preparing plants for next year.

★ Cuttings of fuchsias and geraniums can be taken and rooted, and cinerarias can be got underway.

★ Sow seeds of plants such as mimulus and salpiglossis now.

★ Strawberry plants can be potted now. Grow on in the greenhouse over winter for a spring crop.

FRUIT

★ Blackberries will be cropping this month, and you may still pick raspberries, redcurrants and blackcurrants.

★ The apple harvest is beginning now. Apples are ripe if they will come away from the tree when given a gentle twist.

★ Fruit such as apples, pears and plums can show signs of brown rot, so keep checking regularly. Remove any affected by rot straight away before it affects good fruit nearby.

★ Cut out old fruiting raspberry canes as soon as the harvest is over. Tie the strong young canes in place along wires for next year's crop and remove surplus.

VEGETABLES

★ Rosemary and thyme cuttings can be taken to give them a good start for next year.

★ Even while you are still harvesting this season's crop, you can start sowing for next. Sow spring cabbage seeds in trays now, so that they can be planted out in their final position in September.

★ Winter greens may need some protection. Earth packed up round the stems will help protect them in high winds.

SEPTEMBER GARDEN DIARY

BULBS

★ For drifts of spring-flowering daffodils, scatter the bulbs and plant them where they fall.

★ For Christmas flowering, pot prepared hyacinth or other bulbs. Keep in a cool dark place, free of frost. When 1in shoots show, bring them out. Keep them in a cool place to make them last longer.

SHRUBS AND TREES

★ Prune flowering cherry.

★ Plant container-grown varieties. Dig a hole large enough to take plant and undisturbed soil ball, with 3in to spare all round. Water plant well and remove the container. Sit the plant on a mixture of peat and bone-meal. Fill in the sides with the same mixture.

★ Never stake container shrubs through the root ball. Drive the stake in at an angle, allowing it to face into the prevailing wind.

★ Plant climbers (like clematis, honeysuckle and climbing hydrangea) and wall plants (such as pyracantha, cotoneaster and abutilon).

FLOWERS

★ Dead head roses and tie in new shoots. Spray against black spot and mildew. Prune ramblers by cutting out all old wood. If there's no new growth, prune most of the old wood back, but leave some. Cut the side shoots back to three buds.

★ In the milder South, annuals can be sown now ready for next spring.

★ Remove dead leaves from irises and plant new ones.

★ Dead head the perennials, and trim back dead stems ready for the main clear up which will take place next month.

SEPTEMBER GARDEN DIARY

VEGETABLES

★ Maincrop carrots, beetroot and potatoes should be ready for lifting at this time of year. Store them in a cool, dark place.

★ Sow spinach outdoors to crop next April.

★ Plant spring cabbages 9in apart, leaving 1ft-2ft between the rows.

FRUIT

★ Pick and store ripened apples.

★ Plant strawberries.

★ Order new stock for late autumn planting.

PONDS

★ Make sure that you keep the pond clear of algae.

★ As they die off, remove the leaves from water plants to prevent them rotting in the pond.

★ Remove any leaves from surrounding trees or plants that fall into the pond.

★ Remember to top up the water regularly during any spells of hot weather.

★ Keep the water aerated during hot weather to help the fish breathe.

HERBS

★ Dry herbs for use during the winter. Pick them when they are in the peak of condition, taking care not to bruise them. Dry in bunches in the airing cupboard or some other warm place.

To dry herbs fast, place them between a couple of sheets of kitchen paper and 'cook' them on a low setting in a microwave oven for 1-2 minutes. Turn and 'cook' them for a further minute. Leave the herbs to rest for ten minutes and then store in airtight jars.

OCTOBER GARDEN DIARY

FLOWER BORDERS

★ The main pre-winter tidy up starts. Once the first frosts have killed off the hardy and half hardy annuals, you can remove all the dead growth.

★ Cut back the herbaceous perennials to virtually ground level.

★ Remove the support canes and any netting. Store safely under cover for next year if sound, but discard any that show signs of rotting.

★ Take cuttings of perennials for propagation. Divide any large clumps to increase stock.

★ Plant biennials in the position in which they are to flower next spring.

★ Spray roses against pests and disease.

★ When dahlias are blackened by frost, lift and dry the tubers and store upside down.

SHRUBS

★ Dig over the shrub border to prepare for planting during the dormant season. Add well-rotted compost, and take care no old weed roots remain.

LAWNS

★ Raise the cutting height on the mower.

★ Clear leaves regularly and if possible brush off any dew before cutting.

★ Scarify to remove old cuttings (thatch), and top dress with Autumn Toplawn.

★ Use a worm killer if there are signs of activity.

OCTOBER GARDEN DIARY

should still open up the ventilators.

★ Clean off any white shading you may have applied during the summer.

★ If you use a greenhouse heater during the winter, now's the time to check that it is working satisfactorily.

★ Sow sweet pea seeds in individual pots or trays.

VEGETABLE GARDEN

★ Harvest onions and tie into ropes. Hang in a dry, airy place, and use as required.

★ Clear away all finished crops to prevent disease attacking and spreading to the rest.

★ To prepare vegetable beds for new planting, dig over well, and apply manure. Lime if necessary.

GREENHOUSE

★ Less watering will be necessary now, but if the weather is good enough you

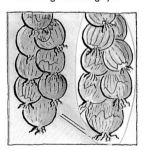

PONDS

★ Water plants will be dying down now, and dead stems should be removed as soon as possible. Rotting vegetation in a pond can cause problems, especially if you have fish.

BULBS

★ Plant bulbs for next summer including iris, crocus, Chiondoxa and tulip.

★ Corms of gladioli should be lifted now, dried and stored in a dry place until next March.

FRUIT

★ Harvest pears and any remaining apples, and store carefully in a cool, dark, slightly ventilated place.

★ Choose and order any new stock.

★ Take hardwood cuttings from currants and gooseberries.

NOVEMBER GARDEN DIARY

FLOWER BORDERS

★ Time to dig the area that you'll be using for next year's annuals. Once dug over roughly, leave alone so that the winter frosts can break it up. If liked, you can add some natural garden compost at this stage.

★ Make sure you have the new seed catalogues. Great for browsing so that you can make your choice and place an order.

★ Finish planting perennials, or leave it until next spring.

LAWNS

★ A final cut may still be possible this month, but it is wise to avoid frosty weather or rain-soaked grass. By this time it'll be necessary to brush off morning dew before cutting.

★ Lay turf, as long as weather is suitable.

★ Prepare soil for seeding grass next spring. Dig and leave for frost to break up.

FRUIT

★ Plant new fruit trees now while soil is still fairly warm.

★ Trees, bushes and canes are pruned between November and March. It's a big subject, so beginners should refer to an instruction book.

VEGETABLES

★ Broad beans can be sown now for next spring. And rhubarb can be planted – allow 1 sq ft for each bud. Sit the bud on top of plenty of manure,

NOVEMBER GARDEN DIARY

with the tip at surface level of the ground.

PONDS

★ Before they rot, remove any leaves that may have dropped into the pond.

★ An early snap of cold weather could ice over the pond. Float a couple of plastic containers on the surface before ice forms, to ensure ventilation holes for fish etc.

BULBS

★ Remove any rotting foliage that may remain round your summer-flowering bulbs.

★ Check over the pots of bulbs that were prepared for Christmas flowering. If growth is showing, take indoors to a light, cool position.

★ Plant tulips this month.

HEATHERS

★ Complete the planting of heathers this month, remembering that they like an acid soil. If yours is not, first prepare the bed with an ericaceous compost.

★ Don't plant heathers in conditions that are frosty, too wet, or over dry.

HEDGES

★ Hedges are decorative, offer privacy, and also provide a windbreak. Plant new deciduous hedges now as long as soil isn't too wet.

★ Don't plant coniferous or evergreen hedges once the weather becomes cold. Leave until next April.

TREES AND SHRUBS

★ Bare-root trees can be planted this month, or next.

★ Container-grown or bare-root deciduous shrubs can be planted now, but leave the evergreens until the spring.

PRIVATE

DECEMBER GARDEN DIARY

ROSES

★ Prepare new beds for planting in February. The soil needs to be left to settle for a couple of months.

★ Clear up any fallen rose leaves and if they show any sign of disease, burn them to eliminate risk of spreading.

★ Check that all the supports for climbers are secure and in good condition to stand up to winter weather.

SHRUBS & HEDGES

★ New, young plants may need protection this year, while becoming established. Provide shelter behind a temporary fence, or cover with straw secured with netting.

★ Continue planting deciduous hedges as long as weather remains suitable. Apply mulch to protect them from frost damage.

★ If any snow falls this month, remember to brush it from the branches as soon as possible to prevent weight damage.

TREES

★ Bare-rooted trees can be planted this month. Remember to place the stake in position on the windward side before planting the tree, or roots may be damaged.

★ Check that stake ties are

secure before weather conditions deteriorate.

BULBS

★ Check the progress of your Christmas bulbs. If well advanced, keep them in a cool position in the house to hold them back for Christmas. If they seem backward, try putting them in a warmer environment to help them on.

GREENHOUSE

★ Make sure the greenhouse heater is working properly –

DECEMBER GARDEN DIARY

you'll need it once the cold weather sets in.

★ If your greenhouse is heated by a paraffin heater, remember to check the fuel level regularly while it's in use.

TOOLS

★ Overhaul equipment ready for next season – all tools should be clean and free of mud. Consider replacing any that are damaged.

★ Clean mower. Check that it is in good running order for next spring and make sure any problems are serviced before

it's put away for the winter.

★ Wash sprayers, watering cans etc in warm soapy water, and dry all the parts carefully before reassembling them to store away.

★ Check the cutting edges of shears, secateurs, knives and other cutting and pruning equipment. Sharpen anything that needs it before you put it away.

★ If your hose is still out, coil it up now and put away in the garage or shed to protect it from frost.

ADVANCE PLANNING

★ Now's the time to think of next summer. So if you want a rockery, pond or new vegetable garden, start drawing up plans.

★ Make your seed selection from catalogues and send off your order. Make sure you work to a plan so that you don't over- or under-order.

INDEX

INDEX

INDEX